# The Revelation of

# Praise
# &
# Worship

## Daphne A. Harris

### Volume Two

WinePress Publishing
MUKILTEO, WA 98275

*Geraldine Dickerson*

**The Revelation of Praise & Worship Vol. 2**
Copyright © 1997 by Daphne Harris

Published by:
Winepress Publishing
P.O. Box 1406
Mukilteo, WA 98275

Cover by Michelle De Monnin for
De Monnin's Art Studio, Milton, WA

Unless otherwise indicated, all scripture is taken from the King James Version of the Bible.

Printed in the United States of America

ISBN 1-57921-055-4
Library of Congress Catalog Card Number: 97-61689

# DEDICATION

This book is dedicated to the memory of my father, the late Dr. Ambrose E. Harris, Jr., for his impact, and strong leadership, demonstrated in my live.

I also dedicate this book to my beloved mother, Mamie Ruth Harris, my brothers, Chalmers, Alonza, Ambrose III, Theophilus, Haldane;  to my sister, Denise, my nieces, Jessica and Jennifer, nephew, Theo Jr., and my sister-in-law, Lisa.

# ACKNOWLEDGEMENT

My special thanks goes to the Holy Spirit who is my most excellent teacher, and my guide into all truth.

Thanks also go out to LaFayette Scales, my pastor, for his tremendous insight, and training in the things of God, and to the Rhema Christian Center Family.

# CONTENTS

# PREFACE

Volume II of "The Revelation of Praise & Worship," has a *heartbeat* of "WORSHIP". This book directs the reader to have close encounters with God. It is written with the intentions of drawing one closer to the Father through intensely worshiping Him. Its aim is to point the reader to make worship a daily practice, that life will abundantly flow from your personal connection with God. The goal of the book is to create a dying hunger, thirst, and passion for God, and His presence as to develop a lasting, abiding relationship with God. The ultimate feature of the book is that once you become engrossed with the Father through worship that you will continue to ascend to different levels, and dimensions in Him. The intent is that there is no limit to the levels or dimensions in Him. They are ceaseless, and have no ending. Therefore, one is to conclude that there will always be another level in worship to transcend unto the Father. There always remains an unveiling of God's character to His people because He is infinite.

Gradually, the book crescendos, and speaks louder and louder to the importance of daily worship. This book begins in the infant stage of worship which creates an unquenching hunger, thirst, and passion for the presence of God. After this passion is birthed in the heart of the reader, then the reader begins to seek the Lord while He may be found. It is Christ in you. Therefore, Christ lives on the inside of us.

After finding the Lord, the reader is admonished to practice daily becoming aware of the presence of God. The reader is then encouraged to receive refreshment, relaxation, and rest from being in His presence. The reader is further encouraged to get to know God by sitting in His presence communicating with the Father, bonding with the Father, playing before the Father, and experiencing new places or realms in His presence as they live daily with Him.

As the book goes on, the reader makes the presence of God their secret place. It becomes a place where God is said to cause the worshiper to conceive of His mind, word, plans, visions, dreams, and revelations as they encounter a very close connection with the Father. This relationship becomes so close that the reader develops intimacy with the Father. A holy communion is also birthed from the intimacy.

In the final stages of the book, the reader is exhorted to come up to higher dimensions in knowing God. They are urged not to be complacent in a comfortable zone, but to ascend to higher levels, and realms of the Spirit through worshiping, and in being intimate with God.

Therefore, the book tells a story from the beginning to the end. It begins generating greater hunger, greater thirst, greater love, and passion in the heart of the worshiper for God. As the worshiper reads on, and travels from one chapter to the other, they encounter communion, deeper fellowship, oneness, and intimacy with God. The worshiper falls in greater love with the Father.

Finally, the latter end of the book deals with the worshiper increasing more and more, soaring, and ascending up to greater, and higher dimensions in worship, and in God. The chapters climb higher and higher, as you read from chapter to chapter. It has a gradual transcendence to them; however, its end is left open to new experiences, new levels, and infinite realms. The latter part of the book has an open end for God to take you to endless levels in Him. It is written so that you are flying high, and are deeply in love with the Father in the end.

The book can also be told as a worshiper searching for God in this country. After finding God, then the worshiper seeks to continue to seek God out by getting a passport and traveling to unknown, infinite, and foreign lands, or places in Him. The worshiper never desires to come back to the place where they started, but is always searching for a new place in God. In addition, the book heightens stages of growing up in God, or advancing to different levels of maturity. Grow in grace, and in the knowledge of our Lord Jesus Christ.

# INTRODUCTION

It is my prayer that you receive breakthroughs into higher dimensions in your walk with God. May you experience new dimensions of hungering and thirsting after Him, knowing Him, seeking Him, sitting before Him, bonding with Him, playing before Him, communing with Him, basking in His presence, being passionated and intimated with Him, loving Him, resting in Him, and worshiping the Father as you journey through this book. God is looking for true worshipers.

May you receive breakthroughs in all areas of your walk with Him: in prosperity, in healing, in resources, in finances, in relationships, in ministry, in visions, in dreams, and in God's purpose for your life. May you also experience new breakthroughs and dimensions in your love for the Father, and His love for you. Most of all, I pray that you experience breakthroughs beyond the veil, into the Father's love chamber, into the Father's secret place, into His Most Holy Place, into new and higher dimensions of God's presence. God desires that you experience His love in greater dimensions that Jesus Christ may be revealed in all of His fulness within you.

Ascend unto Him. Cleave unto Him. Pant after Him. Rapture into His presence. Touch His heart. Seek after Him. Pursue Him. Become intimate with Him. Become one with the Father. Be passionate for Him. Desire Him. Seek to please Him. Increase more and more in Him. Rise up to higher levels. Rise up and worship. Remember, God lives in you. Seek Him from within.

For Almighty God is far greater than our finite minds have the capacity to perceive. He is mightier than we can comprehend mightiness to be. He is richer than our perceptions of richness ever will be. His power extends far beyond all of creation's perception of it. His love reaches deeper than we will ever perceive that it can go. He is wiser than the whole world's wisdom put together. He is bigger than the heavens, the earth, and all things beneath it. His mercy and His grace exceeds our perception of it. He is larger than we will ever fathom Him to be. He is greater than all of our minds together will ever grasp. He modifies Himself so that our finite and limited minds can glimpse God in all His glory, and His infiniteness. Even these words that I am expressing of Him are so limited to the actual description, worth, power, and ability that God has.

For He is phenomenon, and noumenon. He is noumenon in the sense that there are attributes, and parts of God that are beyond description, words, and human language. These descriptions have no words to express God's excellence. That is why there comes a time that we simply stand in extreme awe, and wonder of God.

His name even is ineffable. For the word of God declares that Jesus has a name that no man knows. It is so great, and magnificent that it cannot be uttered, described, or even known. There are parts of God that are unspeakable, indescribable; inexpressible that to know these things would literally blow our minds! For He is God! There is nothing that I can find to compare, or match Him to. For there is nothing beside Him! For He said that there is nothing that He can liken Himself to or to compare Himself with. He is God! And oh the magnitude of His love. His love for you is so awesome that if you really knew its depthness, it will literally, blow your mind.

He is regal, royal, and full of majesty. He is full of jewels, precious stones, colors, riches, wealth, and treasures that we have not perceived. There are jewels in God that we have never seen or heard. He's noble, kingly, and princely, and is enthroned in brilliant, splendid glory! Oh, the riches of His glory! He is God!

So open up to Him. Discover Him. Seek Him. Find Him. Become intimate with Him. Fall in love with Him. Adore Him. Passionately embrace Him. Become intimate with Him. Become one with Him. For this union with Him cannot be broken, or put asunder. For He is thy Husband, and thy Maker. For He is eternal, for He is God. Worship Him! You are greatly loved! Peace!

*Like skim milk is to cream, so praise is to worship.*
*Cream is richer, thicker, and sweeter. Oh,*
*taste and see that it is good!*

*Worship eases heir pressure!*

# CHAPTER ONE

# PASSION FOR HIS PRESENCE

"As the heart **panteth** after the water brooks, so **panteth** my soul after thee, O God." Psalm 42:1

I'm on fire! I'm blazing with anticipation! I'm burning on the inside, waiting for the arrival of a far more than awesome God! I'm enthusiastic! I'm full of zeal! I'm filled with fervor! My heart is awaiting the revelation of the presence of God. My desire is without limit! I hunger and I thirst for the living presence of the living God! I am passionate for God's presence! I'm ready! I'm ready to be consumed by this consuming God! Oh, I'm passionate for His presence!

Then I cry out unto God, "I NEED YOU LORD; CONSUME ME!" "For our God is a consuming fire." Hebrews 12:29. Consume me, that I may consume you!

To consume means that God will totally engulf you with His presence, and with His glory. He desires to give you all of Him. He wants to devour you with His Spirit. He wants to exhaust you, until there is nothing left but what God desires within you. Like a sponge, He wants to consume all of you. He wants your everything. **As you become passionate for Him, you better believe that He is definitely waiting on you with strong passion for you!** God is full of passion, and desires an intimate relationship with you. Cultivate your relationship with Him. Work on it each day. Know that He is waiting to release all of His passion into your heart. Inhale as much of God as you can. Become engrossed with Him. Swallow as much of Him as you can. Consume Him.

To totally be able to consume God, you must first dispose of anything unlike Him that He may have the preeminence in your heart. Let God be the center of attention. Let God be first. Devour Him. Be passionate for the unveiling of all of Him! Stop no where short of it.

Passion is a powerful emotion that leads me to God. The object of my love, hunger, thirst and desire for God is my passion for Him. Passion is an intensity of feeling, such as excitement, warmth, or fervor. It is suffering for the sake of others. Passion for others causes you to be longsuffering for their sake.

Passion knows no bounds. It knows no limits. It has a heartbeat of its own. It is a boundless, enthusiastic, creative, strong love for God. Passion inspires me to pursuit, to craziness, and to strong enthusiasm towards God with zeal. My passion for God propels me into His presence. My passion for God's presence inspires me to worship Him. Worship God with strong passion for Him. Worship Him with passion. Allow your passion to brew on the inside of you, and offer it up to God as a sweet smelling savor. Passionately worship God.

In Psalm 42:1, 'the hart longing for the water brooks', is compared to my heart and my soul longing for the presence of the living God.

Panting means to breathe hard with great desire for something. It is longing demonstratively for something; to yearn for it. Panting is also uttering something hurriedly, or breathlessly. Panting is a craving, a longing for, an intense, strong desire for something! Panting is passion.

We crave God's presence! We long to hear from Him! I long to hear His voice! My soul and my heart cry out to the Living God. Desire to be in His presence. Wait for Him.

He sustains me; and causes me to consist. I long for God. My passion is for His presence. I have an appetite for Him. My passion is to be with Him. My heart cannot wait!

I will never leave you, or forsake you. As the hart **panteth** after the water brooks, so **panteth** my soul after thee, O God.

# Oh Come, Let Us Worship & Bow Down!

*Like bread without yeast is made flat, so is worship without holiness!*

*Worship is our means of pursuing God.*

*Worship produces giants!*

## CHAPTER TWO

# HUNGERING AFTER GOD

"Blessed are they which do hunger and thirst after righteousness: for they shall be filled." Matthew 5:6

"Blessed are ye that hunger now: for ye shall be filled." Luke 6:21

"And Jesus said unto them, I am the bread of life: he that cometh to me shall never hunger; and he that believeth on me shall never thirst." John 6:35

"They shall hunger no more, neither thirst any more; neither shall the sun light on them, nor any heat." Revelation 7:16

### To Never Hunger

Are you hungry? Are you hungry for God? Are you hungry for righteousness? Are you longing for the Word? Well, Jesus said in John 6:35, "I am the bread of life: he that cometh to me shall never hunger...." So, a loaf of Sunbeam bread is not all that we need to hunger for, but you must also hunger for the Bread of Life. "Man shall not live by bread alone, but by every word that proceedeth out of the mouth of God." Matthew 4:4.

In order for me to never hunger again, I must come, or go to Jesus. The word 'cometh' is the Greek word, 'erchomai,' pronounced (er' -khom-ahee). It means to follow after another; or to be established, or to become known publicly. Therefore, when you come to Jesus, you begin to follow after Him, and become established in

Him. When you follow him, this also becomes public. When you come to Jesus, you will never hunger!

To hunger is the Greek word 'peinao,' pronounced (pi –nah'-o). It literally means to suffer want, to be needy, to crave ardently, or to seek with eager desire. To be hungry is to have a strong desire, or need for FOOD! Food is the Word of God! I Peter 2:2 says to desire the sincere milk of the word, that ye may grow thereby. The Word causes you to grow, and it produces life! You will become stronger, and stronger!

Your spirit has a strong desire, or need for God's Word. Your inner man needs to be fed. Your flesh has a strong desire, or need for natural food. Even though the flesh crave food, the Word says that we cannot live by just natural bread alone, but by the Bread of the Word of God. We need every morsel. We must live by every Word. Every word that God speaks, my spirit needs that word for strength, direction, and guidance. We cannot do anything without God.

When you become hungry, this means that you are having discomfort, weakness, or pain which is brought on by the lack of food. When you are physically hungry, your body craves one thing, and that's food! The body does not crave trees, wood, hay, or anything inedible, but the body craves FOOD!

So your spirit craves only one thing, and that's the Word of God! Your body, the flesh, craves natural food, yet the spirit craves spiritual food, the Word of God. Your spirit is not satisfied with anything short of the Word of God. It does not crave the word of man, but the Word of God. It cannot survive with anything other than the Word!

When you crave food, this is a strong wish for what gives your body enjoyment, pleasure, or fulfillment. When the inner man craves the Word, enjoyment, fulfillment, and strength along with many more things are yours to enjoy.

To be hungry for the Word is to need it urgently, or to beg for it earnestly. It can also mean to have an intense desire for. When you are hungry for the Word this means that you have a strong longing for it, as if your spirit within is saying, '*I want that!*'

When you hunger for the Word for your inner man, you yearn for it. You long for it. You desire it and no other. You thirst for it. Your spirit begins to weaken without it.

Without it you cannot do anything! Without it, you become weaken. Without it, you will fail. Without it, you will lose many battles. Without it, you will fall into sin. Without it, the enemy can gain the victory. Without it, you are prone to make wrong decisions, or give out wrong advice. Your strength is small without the Word. Your reactions to different circumstances and situations will even become weakened.

One thing about this is that when you are strong, you react to different things strongly. You make wise, and strong decisions. You have victory. You rebuke, and whatever you are rebuking is bound, and it stops! You lay your hands upon the sick, and the sick recovers! When your inner man is strong because of the Word, temptations will come, yet you will not yield. In these cases, you will choose the way of escape instead of succumbing to sin.

The Word of God in you will heal you! It's like medicine to your body, and to your spirit! "My son, attend to my words; incline thine ear unto my sayings. Let them not depart from thine eyes; keep them in the midst of thine heart. For they are life unto those that find them, and health to all their flesh." Proverbs 4:20-22. That's how powerful the very words of God are! It has multi-functions! The Word of God expresses the mind, will, and heart of God.

"For the word of God is quick, and powerful, and sharper than any two-edged sword, piercing even to the dividing asunder of soul and spirit, and of the joints and marrow, and is a discerner of the thoughts and intents of the heart." Hebrews 4:12.

The word 'quick' in this verse is the Greek word, 'zao,' pronounced (dzah'-o). This word means to live, to breathe, be among the living; not lifeless, or dead. Furthermore, the word 'quick' means to make alive, or to be full of vigor. This word quick also means to spring forth living water. It has vital power in and of itself. To be quick means to be alive, fresh, strong, active, powerful, or to be efficient.

The word of God brings life, abundant life, and vitality. It refreshes your spirit. It brings to your spirit a power that combats all depression, oppression, brokenness, hurt, grief, discouragement, anger, temptation, bitterness, jealousy, a lying tongue, etc. Your spirit is not lifeless, or dead, because the word of God feeds the spirit with power to, and to be how God ordains the spirit to take control over the flesh.

*Worship is sometimes like salt on an open wound,*
*sometimes it hurts to press in, but it heals.*

*Worship moves the heart of God, which moves the hand of God.*

*Worship is like helium blown into a balloon,*
*the balloon will not rise, and soar without it.*

# CHAPTER THREE

# THIRSTING AFTER GOD

"As the hart panteth after the water brooks, so panteth my soul after thee, O God." Psalm 42:1

"My soul longeth, yea, even fainteth for the courts of the LORD: my heart and my flesh crieth out for the living God." Psalm 84:2

"O God, thou art my God; early will I seek thee: my soul thirsteth for thee, my flesh longeth for thee in a dry and thirsty land, where no water is." Psalm 63:1

God to my soul is like water to my body; like water to a deer in a dry, and thirsty land after a very long chase from their predators! Water to my body is very necessary. The water to the deer is a must, lest he faint. I need God: my soul needs Him, my spirit cries out to

Him, and my body clings to Him. My spirit cries out to Him for help, for comfort, for peace, for His missed presence.

"I am the vine, ye are the branches: He that abideth in me, and I in him, the same bringeth forth much fruit: for without me ye can do nothing." John 15:5

To be without God, is to be without air, to be without oxygen, or without breath! God is your oxygen! You need God! In I Corinthians 13:1, it states that you can speak with tongues of men and of angels, and have not charity(love), you become as sounding brass, or a tinkling cymbal. Verse 2 says if you have not charity, you are nothing! So, without God, you can do nothing; and without love, you are nothing, for "God is love." I John 4:8, 16.

When I look around at all that is happening to me, and haunting me, I begin to run to the Father. I run to him for help. I run to him for solutions! I run to Him for answers! I run TO HIM for deliverance, for refreshment, for renewal, for mercy, for grace, for forgiveness, for cleansing, for purging, for love, for companionship, for shelter, for healing, for victory, for a MIRACLE! I begin to realize that I cannot make it without the Lord. I begin to realize that I cannot live by bread alone, but by every word that proceeds out of the mouth of God. I begin to understand that something is missing!

The world is weighing heavy on me! The pressures of my trials are bearing heavy on me! I need comfort. I need rest! I need relief. I need inner healing! I need refreshment for my soul! My soul long for the Lord! My soul is seeking Him! My soul is searching for God! I pant for Him. I long for Him! I desire Him! In Psalm 42:1, "As the hart panteth after the water brooks, so panteth my soul after thee, O God," this verse brings relief to my soul.

### Panting After God

The **hart** in this verse is classified as an animal that is a very fast runner. They are known to run as fast as 64km/h(40mph)! They are full of agility, vigor, energy, pep, and are very active. They have long, slender legs having on its foot two toes tipped by strong, curved hooves. The hart is classified as a clean animal.

Sometimes, harts can be so overwhelmed from thirst as they drink by the water brooks, that they become unaware of their enemies, other animals, predators, or hunters approaching them from behind for attack. When this happens, they are so engrossed with their thirst that someone, or something can literally come so close to the hart before the hart would actually acknowledge, recognize, or flee from their presence.

When harts are being hunted by dogs, or their enemies, they begin to instinctively seek water to bathe their hot, smoking flanks that might give their presence away; and/or to escape the terror of the dogs. They pant for water to escape their enemy, as well as to quench their appetite of thirst for running too long, and too hard!

Our souls, longing for God, are being paralleled with the hart panting, i.e., traveling 40 mph, for the water brook to quench its thirst. The rate at which the hart is traveling is very quickly! Their movements are fast. They bounce, leap, and trot, as they go. Nothing can stop them! Nothing can hinder them! Whatever gets in their way does not become an obstacle, but a stepping stone.

The word "**panteth**" means to long for, to desire, to wish for, to hope for, or to dream of. Panteth can go a bit deeper in its meaning as to go beyond desiring, or longing for, but to desire to the extent as one who is out of breath, or breathing very hard. When you pant, your breathing is done rapidly in short gasps, as if you have forcefully exerted yourself. It is as if you are running so hard, and so long that you become tired, and out of breath.

You give off loud puffs, especially while you're moving! Your heart is beating loudly, and heavily. You're out of breath! You are inhaling, and exhaling, rapidly! You are breathing convulsively, and laboriously! You are blowing very hard; heaving, puffing, huffing, gasping, blowing, and panting!

"Lord, Lord, Lord, Lord, where are you! Lord, Lord, I need you; Lord, Lord, Lord, I desire you, and no other! Lord, Lord, Lord, I want to worship You, for you alone are God(huff, huff, puff, puff)! I bow before you! I humble myself before you Lord, show me thy GLORY; show me thy face!"

You are giving it all you have! You are bowed down, crouched down on your knees. You are prostrated before Him. Tears are rolling down your cheeks! You are there, in the presence of the Lord! ......then He speaks; He comforts you; He consoles you. He strengthens you, He upholds, and holds you, He woos you closer, He grants unto you wisdom, and joy. "Thou wilt shew me the path of life: in thy presence is fulness of joy; at thy right hand there are pleasures for evermore." Psalm 16:11

Another common definition for "**panteth**," is to '*bray*'. To bray is to utter loud, harsh cries. It is to sound loudly, and harshly. *To bray* is to make sounds similar to that of a donkey. From this definition, I see one's soul, and heart crying out unto the Lord. From the depths of their being, from the center of their existence, from the bottom of their heart, their soul is resounding loudly, unto the Lord.

In Psalm 16:11, stated above, God's **presence** is the Hebrew word, "*paniym*," pronounced *paw-neem'*. It means the face of God; which is the immediate proximity in time or space. The presence of God depicts, or proves His actual current, immediate existence! "*Paniym*"(**presence**) also means in front of, before, to the front of, in the presence of, in the face of, at the face or front of, from the presence of, from before, from before the face of, or *presence* simply means **here**, or **right now**.

The word "fulness" in this verse means an abundance, or satiety. Satiety means the condition of being full or gratified beyond the point of satisfaction; surfeit. Surfeit is to feed or supply to excess. It is also defined as a condition of going, doing, or being beyond what is needed, desired, or appropriated. It's having a surplus, excess, an overabundance, or superabundance of something!

Joy is the Hebrew word "simchah" pronounced "sim-khaw'." It is defined in the Hebrew language as gladness, mirth, having glad results, or experiencing happy issues. When joy is experienced one is made glad, i.e., you are pleased, cheerful, appreciative, delighted, merry, happy, or festive. In God's presence you receive delight, and provision from Him. Therefore, everything that you need is definitely supplied in His presence.

You have joy even in trials, and tribulations. The joy is there because you realize that God sees you in your dilemma, and will help you. "Many are the afflictions of the righteous, but the Lord delivereth him out of them all." Psalm 34:19.

In God's presence is everything you need. There comes a time when you come into the presence of God to partake with Him; to sup with Him; and to worship Him. In worshiping Him, there is no need of asking God for your daily needs, for in His presence you have the fulness of joy, and at His right hand pleasure forevermore.

You receive wisdom in His presence, as you worship Him. You receive love, freedom, victory, empowerment, solutions, answers, healing, deliverance; miracles begin to happen.

Abundance is yours, but you will find it in His presence. The superabundance harvest is yours, but get in His presence! Stay there. Become acquainted with the Father. Learn of Him! Rest from all your wearies as you begin to learn how to dwell in His presence. All things are yours!

### Quenching Your Thirst

*"There cometh a woman of Samaria to draw water: Jesus saith unto her, Give me to drink. (For his disciples were gone away unto the city to buy meat.) Then saith the woman of Samaria unto him, How is it that thou, being a Jew, askest drink of me, which am a woman of Samaria? for the Jews have no dealings with the Samaritans. Jesus answered and said unto her, If thou knewest the gift of God, and who it is that saith to thee, Give me to drink; thou wouldest have asked of him, and he would have given thee living water. The woman saith unto him, Sir, thou hast nothing to draw with, and the well is deep: from whence then hast thou that living water? Art thou greater than our father Jacob, which gave us the well, and drank thereof himself, and his children, and his cattle? Jesus answered and said unto her,*

Whosoever drinketh of this water *shall thirst* again: But whosoever drinketh of the water that I shall give him *shall never thirst;* but the water that I shall give him shall be in him a well of water springing up into everlasting life.

*The woman saith unto him, Sir,* give me this water, that I thirst not, neither come hither to draw......

*Jesus saith unto her, Woman, believe me, the hour cometh, when ye shall neither in this mountain, nor yet at Jerusalem,* worship the Father. *Ye worship ye know not what: we know what we worship: for salvation is of the Jews. But the hour cometh, and now is, when the* true worshipers shall worship the Father in spirit and in truth: *for the Father* seeketh *such to worship him.*

God is *a* Spirit: and they that worship him must worship him in *spirit and in truth....*The woman then left her waterpot, and went her way into the city, and saith to the men,

Come, see a man....and they went out of the city, and came unto him." John 4:7-30

The Samaritan woman described in this story was primarily considered to be a poor woman. It is surmised that she was poor in that most women no longer had to come and draw water at wells, for this was considered an ancient custom, or tradition. During this time, only the poor had to still come and draw water from the well. This woman was also described as being degrading, and an adulteress.

This well, where the woman came to fetch a pot of water (called Jacob's well), was about 105 ft. deep, 9 ft. in diameter, an area of 64 square feet, and had 15 ft. of water. The well was cut out of solid rock, and showed the engineering skill of ancient biblical times.

In this passage, the Samaritan woman went to the well to seek water. It was accustomed that young men who sought to marry a woman would come here to meet them. As a result in this story, Jesus became that man in the Samaritan woman's heart to join up with her, to unite with her, and to spiritually marry her. It was also accustomed that eastern travelers frequently carry a leather bucket to the well with them, to draw water from public wells.

At the time of the woman's encounter with Jesus, it was the sixth hour (12 noon). At this time of the day, it was very hot. During this time, there would be no travelers on the road, neither would there be women at the well. The women generally came early in the morning, or late in the evening at sunset, to draw water.

Jesus offered her a drink. His drink was described as living water. Living water is defined as *"life-giving, or life breathing"* water. Life-giving water gives life, eternal life. This eternal life will never perish. Therefore, if I drink of the living water that Jesus offered the Samaritan woman, it will last for more than a life time, but throughout all eternity.

When Jesus stated that He had water that would cause you to never thirst, he was alluding to the woman partaking of Himself. He had living water that would cause the woman to live forever.

This living water will cause your soul, and spirit to have life, and strength forever. Once you receive this living water, you do not have to come back and get another dose. As the Samaritan woman would have to return on the next day to get another dip for her thirst, this is not necessary in the spirit realm. In the spirit realm, living water is equated to receiving salvation(vs. 13, 14). You receive Jesus Christ once and for all. In receiving salvation, it is enough to last for a lifetime, for all eternity! This kind of water quenches your thirst forever. This type of living water quenches your soul forever. The soul becomes satisfied, pleased, suited, and fulfilled.

"**Blessed** are they which do hunger and **thirst** after righteousness: *for they shall be filled.*" Matthew 5:6

**To thirst** after God, and His righteousness **means** to have a keen, eager, ardent, famishing, all-consuming craving, and passion of the soul for complete union with God and the fullness of the Spirit. *The word thirst is the Greek word "***dipsao***" pronounced* (dip-sah'-o). **Dipsao means** to suffer thirst; or to have a painful feeling of want of, or eagerly longing for those things by which the soul is refreshed, supported, and strengthened.

In John 7:37, "If any man thirst, let him come unto me, and drink," **to come unto Jesus means** to completely surrender your life unto Jesus to do the entire will of God as He reveal it unto you. **When you drink, it means** that you wholeheartedly receive into your heart and life the gifts, fruit, desires, and operations of the Holy Spirit of God. *To drink* means to accept what the Spirit has to offer, and to obey by applying what the Spirit speaks.

FILL MY CUP, LORD

### LIVING WATER

*Living water* is water from the fountain of heaven. It is water from the spirit of God. It is water that causes a person to do more than just live in their flesh, but it causes the spirit, the inner man, to live. In verse 4, *living* is the *Greek* word "**zao**," pronounced (dzah'-o). **Zao** means in the Greek language: to live, breathe, be among the living, to enjoy real life, to find life, to have true life, to be active, blessed, and endless in the kingdom of God. It also means to have vital power in itself to the exerting of the same upon the soul. Zao is also defined as being full of vigour; to be fresh, strong, efficient, active, powerful, and efficacious.

**Water** produces $\longrightarrow$ life

**Living water** produces $\longrightarrow$ everlasting life

Water causes things to grow, and eventually those things die; but living water causes things to not just grow, but to grow, and live forever and ever. Water has a nourishing power, and is limited; but **living water** not only nourishes but **empowers, quickens, resurrects, strengthens, and anoints!** Living water that Jesus gives is of an enduring and abiding nature which will continue to satisfy the heart, day by day, moment by moment, hour by hour.

If living water springs forth everlasting life, then this water is everlasting, abiding, lasting, and enduring. It is also mentioned in the Old Testament prophecies as good things to come.

It is stated in Isaiah 12:3, "Therefore with joy shall **ye draw water out of the wells of salvation."**

"I will **pour water upon him that is thirsty**, and **floods** upon the dry ground: I will **pour my Spirit upon thy seed**, and **my blessing upon thine offspring."** Isaiah 44:3

"In that day there shall be **a fountain opened** to the house of David and to the inhabitants of Jerusalem for sin and for uncleanness."

"And it shall be in that day, that **living waters shall go out** from Jerusalem; half of them toward the former sea, and half of them toward the hinder sea: in the summer, and in the winter shall it be." Zechariah 14:8

In John 7:38, "He that believeth on me, as the scripture hath said, **out of his belly** shall **flow rivers** of **living water**," notice the term living water. First of all, the word belly is the Greek word "koilia" pronounced (koy-lee'-ah). **Koilia** means the whole belly; the womb, the place where the fetus is conceived and nourished until birth; or the innermost part of a man, the soul and the spirit, the seat of the intellect, emotions, and desires; the heart of man's innermost being as the seat of thought, feeling, and choice. The belly is where the word is conceived. It is a place where revelation knowledge is conceived by the Spirit, before it is poured out and shared. It is known to be the midst of man. **Once the word is conceived by the Spirit within the spirit man, out comes living water.**

Flow is the Greek word, "rheo," pronounced (hreh' -o). It means to move or run smoothly with unbroken continuity. Flow also means to issue; pour forth; to proceed steadily and easily; to arise; or to abound in motion. The word in the belly will be released to flow smoothly, accomplishing, being steadfast in its motion. The word will proceed forth from the belly steadily, and easily. It will arise in the belly, or heart and come forth as pure gold. It will arise and accomplish. It will arise and give birth. It will arise and produce. It will arise and pour itself forth into the hearts and minds of the people. When the word goes forth, it will prosper, deliver, set free, heal, live, and impart life. The word will arise, and thus abound in what it set out to do. To abound means to be fully supplied, filled, or to be in great amounts, or numbers. The word will abound in richness, wealth, power, grace, might, and spirit.

When the word goes forth, it will not travel in motion as a seed, or word, but will go forth already pregnant with other seeds. It goes forth pregnant into the minds and hearts of the people so that it can bear, and produce more fruit. Every time something, or someone is born, there is already seed planted within that seed.

**Rivers** is the Greek word, "potamos," pronounced (pot-am-os'). It too has the implication of a flooding, swifting-flowing stream. It also implies a heavy downpour, or a heavy uncontrollable outpouring. Out of the belly shall flow an uncontrollable outpouring of the word, and Spirit. The outpouring is so heavy, and overflowing that it has power to cause one to begin to **speak in tongues, prophesy, preach, dream dreams, and see visions.**

### An Outpouring

Joel 2:28 states, "And it shall come to pass afterward, that I will **pour out** my Spirit upon all flesh; and your sons and your daughters *shall prophesy*, your old men *shall dream dreams*, your young men *shall see visions*: And also upon the servants and upon the handmaids in those days will I **pour out** my spirit." Acts 2:17 states, "And it shall come to pass in the last days, saith God, I will **pour out** of my Spirit upon all flesh: and your young men *shall see visions*, and your old men *shall dream dreams*: And on my servants and on my handmaidens I will **pour out** in those days of my Spirit; and they *shall prophesy....*"

From the belly of God, from His innermost being will He pour out upon His sons, daughters, young men, old men, servants, and handmaidens, His Spirit. After the pouring, then the prophesying.

After the pouring then the dreams. After the pouring then the visions. Let it rain 'Spirit!' Let the Spirit pour!

To pour out in the Greek is the word "ekcheo," pronounced (ek-kheh'-o). It means to shed forth. It also means to bestow, or distribute largely. To pour out is the Hebrew word, "shaphak," pronounced (shaw-fak'). It means to spill, shed, to send forth, produce, express, or to flow in a steady stream. This word 'pour' means to flow **continuously, or profusely.** It means to **rain hard,** or to **pour out heavily. A pouring out of something is like serving a beverage, such as tea or coffee, at a gathering! In contrast, a pouring out of the Spirit is a heavy serving of the powers of the Spirit unto and into the people of God at a gathering, worship service, or while alone!**

To pour out also means a giving out of oneself. This pouring out is illustrated in Philippians 2:7 which states, "....But made himself(Jesus) of no reputation, and took upon him the form of a servant, and was made in the likeness of men." The word *reputation* is the Greek word "kenoo," pronounced (ken-o'-o). **Kenoo means to empty, or to make empty.** Jesus emptied Himself as He poured out Himself! As Jesus Christ shed His blood on Calvary's rugged cross, He was pouring out Himself, or emptying Himself.

**Pouring out is also illustrated in Galatians 4:4 which states, "But when the fulness of the time was come, God sent forth His Son, made of a woman, made under the law." When God sent forth His Son, He was actually pouring out Himself into the world. Therefore it can be concluded that God was pouring out Himself unto His people.**

He pours out Himself as if He's rain unto His people. He's rain to bring life. He's rain to bring productivity. Jesus is rain to bring resurrection. He's rain to bring growth. He's rain to bring growth from one level of glory to another. He's rain to bring forth abundant fruit. He's rain to bring forth more, and much fruit. He's rain to bring forth the harvest. He's rain to bring forth the wealth. He's rain to bring forth eternal life. He's rain to bring forth life more abundantly.

John 10:10 states, "The thief cometh not, but for to steal, and kill, and to destroy: I am come that they might have life, and that they might have it more abundantly."

**To have life more abundantly** is to have life exceedingly with great measure. It means to have something over and above what you need, more than what is necessary; superadded, or supremely. To have something more abundantly also means to have much more than all; to be superior, extraordinary, surpassing, uncommon, or to be pre-eminent. You have the advantage if you have something more abundantly. There is a high degree of excellence.

**THERE SHALL BE SHOWERS OF BLESSINGS!**
**WHEN IT RAINS, IT POURS!**

### Jesus, Thirsting for His Father's Presence

In John 19:28, it is recorded, "After this, Jesus knowing that all things were now accomplished, that the scripture might be fulfilled, saith, 'I THIRST'." In this passage, Jesus is not literary thirsting for drink, but He is longing for His Father from within. Jesus was eagerly awaiting reunion with His father. He longed for His father. He thirsted for Him.

### A Word in Season for...
### Those Who Lack Thirst for God

In Jesus' Name....I pray that those who lack thirst for God, would ask Him to give unto you a thirst that is unquenchable! May you sincerely thirst after God. May you sincerely **thirst after His presence, His will, His mind, His heart, His purpose, His plan, His path, and His Word.**

May you strongly desire to drink from the fountain of His Word, that you will grow thereby. May your thirst for God be with vigour, and unfailing desire. May you ascend unto God. May you look unto the hills from whence cometh your help. May you reach, and touch the heart of God.

### May you desire God's presence above all others.

May you yearn for His presence. May your heart pant for the Holy of Holies by way of the Holy Place; may your heart pant after God to dwell with Him, to abide with Him, and to enjoy His atmo

You have the power....You have the anointing....You have the Word....You have the blood of Jesus....You have the authority....You have dominion to dominate in your spirit!

**Break through, that you may receive breakthroughs!**
Discard whatever is unlike Him. Those things which God hates,
you hate. Those things which God loves, you love. **Be like Him.**
Desire to be His reflection. Desire to be what He made you to
be. Desire to reach the potential that He has ordained you to reach.
Desire to reach, and finish the goal set before you. Establish your
position, and right of your inheritance.
Yearn for it. Desire it.

**Thirst for what God made you to be.**
Do not thirst for things of the world. Do not thirst for material
possessions, but thirst for God for He is enduring! Do not thirst for
any type of drink, but the drink of the Holy Ghost! Do not thirst
for fleshy desires, but thirst to please God.

You may thirst....
for strong drink, it will never satisfy;
for immortality, it will never satisfy;
for drugs, they will never satisfy;
for wild parties, they will never satisfy;
for big money, it will never satisfy;
for top positions, it will never satisfy;
for a good high, it will never satisfy;
for a good time, it will never satisfy;
for a quick fix, it will never satisfy;

ONLY JESUS WILL AND CAN COMPLETELY SATISFY YOU!
SINCE I WAS CREATED IN THE IMAGE OF GOD, HE MADE
ME SO THAT HE AND ONLY HE CAN SATISFY ME. MAN
CANNOT BE SATISFIED UNTIL HIS HEART IS RIGHT WITH
GOD!

**Your thirst for other things is really a thirst for God! It's a
signal that says, "I need God!"**
Let your heart pant after God. Let your heart pant for His
presence. Seek to please God. For without faith, it is impossible
to please the Father!
In the morning, seek Him. In the noon day, seek Him. In the
evening, and night, seek God.

Hear His waters flowing.  Hear the waters falling.  Hear the waters splashing.  Hear the waters singing.

**Thirst for Him.**
And ye shall seek me and find me when ye have searched with all your heart.
When you seek after God, so thirsty for Him,
YOU WILL FIND HIM...YOU WILL BE ARRESTED, IN HIS PRESENCE!  HE WILL MANIFEST HIMSELF TO YOU.  YOU WILL HEAR, AND KNOW HIS VOICE.  YOU WILL HAVE NO FEAR.  YOU WILL FEEL HIS LOVE FOR YOU, HIS JOY, HIS FULNESS.
**YOU WILL BE FILLED!**
BLESSED ARE THOSE WHO HUNGER, AND THIRST AFTER RIGHTEOUSNESS,
**FOR THEY SHALL BE FILLED!**
YOU WILL SENSE HIS PRESENCE!  YOU WILL FEEL HIS PRESENCE!
YOU WILL KNOW THAT YOU HAVE BEEN WITH GOD!  YOU WILL BE PLEASED!  YOU WILL BE SATISFIED!  YOU WILL BE BLESSED, AFTER FINDING GOD!
**HE WILL BE ALL YOU NEED, AND THEN SOME!**
ABUNDANCE WILL BE YOURS!  THE HARVEST IS YOURS! PROVISION IS YOURS!  THERE WILL BE NO LACK!  HE IS ALL YOU NEED!
OH, TASTE AND SEE THAT THE LORD IS GOOD!  SIP! DRINK! TASTE!  TASTE HIS GOODNESS!  TASTE HIS AFFECTION AND HIS WARMTH FOR YOU!  TASTE HIS LOVE!  TASTE HIM. CHEW WHAT YOU GET!  DIGEST IT!  IT'LL BE HEALTH TO YOUR MARROW.  NUTRITION TO YOUR SPIRIT!  FEEL HIS EMBRACE.  FEEL HIS TOUCH!
FILL MY CUP LORD, I LIFT IT UP LORD.
GOD IS FAITHFUL TO HIS WORD!  HE WILL DO AND BE WHAT HE SAID HE WILL BE!
THERE IS NO LACK, OR DEFICIENCY IN GOD!  YOU WILL BE SURPRISED ONCE YOU DWELL IN HIS PRESENCE!
**GET THERE.......HE'LL HOOK YOU UP!**
WHEN YOU DO NOT KNOW WHAT TO PRAY FOR AS YOU OUGHT, PRAY IN THE SPIRIT....THE SPIRIT OF GOD WILL

MAKE UTTERANCES FOR YOU THAT WILL BLOW YOUR
MIND! THE SPIRIT OF GOD WILL SEARCH THE MIND OF
GOD, AND MEET YOUR EVERY NEED. TRY IT, YOU'LL SEE!
TRY IT, YOU'RE LIKE IT!
ALL THINGS ARE YOURS! YOU ARE A JOINT HEIR TO THE
THRONE OF GOD! THE INHERITANCE BELONGS TO YOU!
RECEIVE IT. BELIEVE IT. IT'S YOURS!
As the deer panteth after the water brook, so panteth your soul
after the Almighty One. Reach for God, and you will find Him.
"DRAW NIGH TO GOD, AND HE WILL DRAW NIGH TO YOU."
James 4:8. Thirst for God. Become so thirsty for Him, that
nothing else will satisfy you. Everything else will fall short of
satisfaction. Look for Him; wait for Him; hope for Him; antici-
pate Him; desire Him; beseech Him; beckon Him;
embrace Him; feel Him; summons
HIS PRESENCE!
Expect Him! Live in expectancy!
"They shall not hunger nor thirst; neither shall the heat nor sun
smite them: for he that hath mercy on them shall lead them,
even by the springs of water shall he guide them." Isaiah 49:10
"Therefore if thine enemy hunger, feed him! if he thirst, give
him drink: for in so doing thou shalt heap coals of fire on his
head." Romans 12:20
"Blessed are they which do hunger and thirst after righteousness: for they shall be filled." Matthew 5:6

Yearn.
Desire.
Be Eager.
Crave.
Touch.
Embrace.
Hear.
Listen.
Obey.
Ask!
Seek.
Find.
Search.

Look.
Press.
Push.
Pant.
Long for.
Commune.
Praise.
Worship.
Fellowship.
Reach.
Ask!
Wait!
Believe!
Hunger!
**THIRST!**

Behold, I will do a new thing!

**I'M TRULY THIRSTY!**
**AMEN.**

*Worship is like flying a kite; the more you let go of the string,*
*the higher you will rise unto the heavens.*

*Like faith without works is dead,*
*worship without the beauty of holiness is dead.*

*Worship is our ears to hear the Spirit of God.*

# CHAPTER FOUR

# SEEKING THE LORD

**"And ye shall seek me, and find me, when ye shall search for me with all your heart." Jeremiah 29:13.**

Oh, the tremendous benefits found in seeking the Lord. "Seek ye the LORD while he may be found, call ye upon him while he is near." Isaiah 55:6. Seeking the Lord means that you look for Him until you find Him. Seeking the Lord implies desiring to be in the presence of God. You seek the Lord in order to find Him. God is near.

"Ask, and it shall be given you; **seek**, and ye shall find; knock, and it shall be opened unto you." Matthew 7:7. In this verse, to seek means to search in order to find out something either by thinking, meditating, reasoning, or inquiring about something. Seeking also is defined as craving, or hungering for something, or someone. It is demanding something from someone, and not leaving or departing until you have received what you were seeking for. This definition is the Greek word, "zeteo."

**When I seek for God, I am in pursuit of Him.** When I hunger and thirst after God, it causes me to be in pursuit of God. I begin to pursue Him. When I pursue, and seek the Lord and find Him, one way that I know when I have found Him, is if my needs, or requests have been met. If I come away from the presence of God having an answer to my unique situation then I have definitely found the Lord. If I come away from the presence of God with a word from heaven, insight from the throne room, fresh manna, fresh bread, a fresh word, visions or dreams for the future, revelations, sharper discernment, or wisdom for my situation, then you must agree that I found my Lord.

If you find yourself still on a search for God and have not yet found Him, then try pursuing Him with **all** your heart. For the scriptures declare.... "And ye shall seek me, **and find me**, when ye shall search for me with all your heart." Jeremiah 29:13. **God is on the inside of you!** Remember, it is Christ **in me**, the hope of glory. Put your whole being into the search for your Lord. Give your all in search for Him, all of your might, all of your strength, power, and all of your heart. Be diligent! Fast, not for your burdens to be lifted, but to seek, and search for God, until you recognize His presence from within. Let's fast in pursuit of God!

When you search for Him with all your heart, there lies a promise to you. The promise is that you will definitely find God. You will hear Him whisper within your heart. Listen for Him. Listen for His voice. Remember, He is gentle. Wait upon Him for Him to speak. Long for Him. Hunger and thirst for Him. Seek Him. Search for Him. And as you search for Him, search the scriptures. Search the scriptures to know God, to find out things about Him. Experience God's throne. Learn of Him. Experience God's presence. Experience God's voice. Search from the bottom of your heart. Search with all of your heart, mind, soul, and strength. Search the scriptures!

"**Search** the **scriptures**; for in them ye think ye have eternal life: and they are they which testify of me." John 5:39.

"Come unto me, all *ye* that labor and are heavy laden, and I will give you rest. Take my yoke upon you, and **learn** of **me**; for I am meek and lowly in heart: and ye shall find rest unto your souls. For my yoke *is* easy, and my burden is light." Matthew 11:29.

### Where God Will Be Found
"To whom God would make known what is the riches of the glory of this mystery among the Gentiles; **which is Christ in you,** the hope of glory." Colossians 1:27.

Please understand that after all of the seeking and searching, that Christ will be found on the inside of you. It is Christ in you, the hope of glory!

Therefore, you do not have to travel across the world looking for God. Know of a surety that Christ resides on the inside of you. **He is in you.** "Abide in me, and I in you." John 15:4.

**God is everywhere! He is omnipresent!**

### Advantages and Disadvantages in Seeking God
In the Book of II Chronicles, there are lives, and characters of those in leadership displayed from chapter to chapter. Notice the character of some of these leaders as they are depicted as one who sought the Lord, or as one who turned from Him.

In II Chronicles 14, Asa did good and right in the eyes of the LORD. He tore down idolatry, and commanded Judah to seek the Lord. In verse 7, because he commanded the people to seek the Lord, God gave them rest on every side from all their enemies. They began to build for themselves cities and villages, and they prospered greatly.

In II Chronicles 17, Jehoshaphat sought the Lord and not Baalim. Because he sought the Lord, the Lord established the kingdom in his hand; and he began to possess riches and honor in abundance. Jehoshaphat's heart was lifted up in the ways of the LORD; and he also began to tear down idolatry worship. He prepared his heart to seek the LORD. II Chron. 19:3.

In II Chronicles 26, Uzziah did that which was right in the sight of the LORD. He sought God, and as long as he sought the LORD, God made him to prosper greatly. II Chron. 26:5. So again, seeking the LORD will cause you to prosper greatly in all things that you do.

In II Chronicles 27, Jotham did that which was right in the sight of God. Therefore, God made Jotham mighty, because he prepared his ways before the LORD, his God, and sought after Him. II Chron. 27:6. If you seek the LORD, God will make you mighty, and will send His prosperity, favor, and peace your way!

On the other hand, in II Chron. 12, Rehoboam did evil in the sight of the LORD, because he **prepared not** his heart to seek the LORD. II Chron. 12:14. Because he sought not the LORD, he automatically did evil in God's sight. What a lesson to learn from this character, and personality!

In II Chron. 20, Jehoshaphat joined himself with wicked Ahaziah to make ships to go to Tarshish. Because Jehoshaphat made an alliance with this wicked king of Israel, God was very displeased. It was prophesied beforehand that their ships would be broken; so they were not able to follow through with their plans to go to Tarshish. In this case, Jehoshaphat did not seek God in his business affairs, or in choosing his business partner, so his plan went down the drain. Seek the LORD! It's better, and more prosperous that way. Your plans will be God's plans, your business partner chosen will be God's choice; and things will definitely prosper!

In chapter21, Jehoram did wickedly, and sought not the LORD. "Behold, with a great plague will the LORD smite thy people, and thy children, and thy wives, and all thy goods: And thou *shalt have* great sickness by disease of thy bowels, until thy bowels fall out by reason of the sickness day by day." II Chron. 21:14, 15. Jehoram was smitten by God in his intestines with an incurable disease. At the end of two years, his intestines fell out by reason of the sickness, and he died. Jehoram sought not the LORD. We must learn how to seek God, because it ensures happiness, prosperity, favor, abundance, wisdom, righteousness, wealth, and good health!

These are key verses on seeking the LORD, that make key points. One verse that stands out in my mind is II Chron. 12:14. Rehoboam did evil in the sight of the Lord. There was a reason given in why Rehoboam did evil in the eyes of God. The reason being that he prepared NOT his heart to seek the LORD. Wow! Woe!

To prepare your heart is to make your heart ready to seek God. It is fixing your mind towards seeking God. It is making arrangements in your schedule according to the Hebrew definition. It is getting ready to meet God, before seeking Him, and knowing that you will find Him from within. It is settling within yourself that this is what you are going to do and sticking with it. Preparing your heart is also causing your heart, and your mind to endure through the process of seeking, searching, and finding Him. Keep your vow to God, seek Him!

In this passage of scripture, to seek the Lord means a number of similar things. It means to resort to, to search carefully, inquiring of God's presence. It means to tread a place, resorting there, until your mission, and purpose have been accomplish in your pursuit of God. Seeking God means to consult with God. It is investigating God's whereabouts, ways, attributes, and His character. Seeking is practicing, studying, following, and searching with application. Jesus said to come unto Him to learn of Him.

"And ye shall seek me, and find me, when ye shall search for me with all your heart." Jeremiah 29:13. "Seek ye the LORD while he may be found, call ye upon him while he is near." Isa. 55:6.

"And ye shall seek me, and find me, when ye shall search for me with all your heart." Jeremiah 29:13. " Draw nigh to God, and he will draw nigh to you. Cleanse *your* hands, *ye* sinners; and purify *your* hearts, *ye* double minded." James 4:8. Seek the Lord, and you will prosper!

### In Search of the Lost Coin

"Either what woman having ten pieces of silver, if she lose one piece, doth not light a candle, and **sweep the house**, and **seek diligently till she find it**? And when she hath found *it*, she calleth *her* friends and *her* neighbors together, saying, Rejoice with me; for I have found the piece which I had lost." Luke 15: 8-9.

Imagine this **lost coin** representing the Father, your health, a lost job, a lost friend, a lost relationship, a lost inheritance, a lost treasure, or a lost fortune. So after it is lost, you begin to search madly for it. You begin to search for the Father, search for that good health, search for a cure, search for that job, that lost friend, that lost relationship, that lost inheritance, that lost treasure, that lost fortune.

The coin was precious to this woman. In order to receive your blessing, you must do what the lady did in this story. **You must light your candle, and sweep your house.** You must light your candle, and clean your house. You must light your candle, and search for your lost coin **until you find it!** You must let your light shine. Imagine your fortune, wealth, prosperity, abundance, or finances being lost like the coin was lost in the story. Therefore, the coin is symbolic of a lost, precious, chosen treasure that she once possessed. The house in which the woman lost her coin is symbolic of your spiritual house!

Imagine your house being your body, your temple. "What? know ye not that your **body** is the **temple** of the Holy Ghost *which is* in you, which ye have of God, and ye are not your own?" I Cor. 6:19.
**Clean your house! Clean your temple house! Clean your spiritual house! Clean up the garbage in your heart; clean up, and sweep out the lust of your heart and mind. Flush the garbage out of your mind, especially, the fantasies. Clean up the idle, corrupted words that come out of your mouth. Clean your ear gate that the only thing you hear is what is pleasing to the Lord. Watch what you hear. Guard your ears. Guard what you hear through the television, or radio.** *Try to cut television out of your schedule completely!*
**Wash your hands, that is, wash or stop the evil, and wrong doings that you do with your hands. Rinse your eyes. Watch what you look at. Watch what you lust after, it may entrap you. Clean your house!**
"Create in me a clean heart, O God; and renew a right spirit within me." Psalm 51:10. "Cleanse thou me from secret *faults*." Psalm 19:12. "Wash me thoroughly from mine iniquity, and cleanse me from my sin." Psalm 51:2. "Purge me with hyssop, and I shall be clean: wash me, and I shall be whiter than snow." Psalm 51:7. "Then will I sprinkle clean water upon you, and ye shall be clean: from all your filthiness, and from all your idols, will I cleanse you." Ezekiel 36:25. "Cleanse *your* hands, ye sinners; and purify *your* hearts, *ye* double minded." James 4:8. "If we confess our sins, he is faithful and just to forgive us *our* sins, and to cleanse us from all unrighteousness." I John 1:9. Confess your sins! Ask for forgiveness. Repent! Clean your house!

Clean your house!  Clean your temple!  Cleanse yourself that you may find the Father.  " **Be ye holy**; for I am **holy**." I Peter 1:16.

Clean up!  The coin that was lost will only be found **if you diligently search for it**; however, in searching for this most valued possession, you must sweep the entire house out in order to find it.  Search for that which you cannot find, or see.  Seek for that most precious, valuable possession!  But notice that you just do not seek for your prize, but you seek diligently for it.  To be diligent is to be persistent, and to persevere.  You search diligently, yes, but do not give up your search until you find what you are looking for.

The coin can also be depicted as your wealth, your prosperity, your riches, or your money.  Before you receive this wealth, this prosperity, or this money, you must clean up your house.  When your house is clean, then you will find your wealth.  When you finish cleaning up your house, you will find what you have lost.  When you have completely searched your premises diligently, and have done a thorough spring cleaning, you will find your riches.  When you seek, and seek, and seek for that which you have lost, what you use to have, you will find your most precious possession, but not until the house is clean.

The key is to seek until you find.  The key is to not give up what you are looking for.  The key is to not abandon your search.  The key is to be faithful in the cleaning.  The key is to not abort the plan in cleaning.  The key is to not abort the mission, your purpose, or your destiny.  The key is to be diligent, steadfast, and unmovable with your task.  The key is to clean, clean, clean and clean.  Accomplish your mission.  Stay focused!  Stay on task.  Go forward, and not backward.  Do it the way God said do it.  In order to receive, CLEAN!  "But they hearkened not, nor inclined their ear, but walked in the counsels *and* in the imagination of their evil heart, and went **backward**, and not forward." Jeremiah 7:24. Clean your house!

Whatever you have lost can be retrieved again.  Whatever you have lost can be found again.  Whatever, or whomever you have lost can be located, and enjoyed again.  Do not give up!  It may take time, but the victory, and deliverance is yours!

Expect to find it!  Expect a miracle to happen!  Expect healing!  Expect prosperity!  Expect victory!  Expect an increase! Expect the inheritance!  Expect an abundance!  Expect to reap!  Expect the harvest! Expect an outpouring! Expect people to be baffled when you find it! Expect God's presence to open unto you! Expect the heavens to open unto you! Expect God to speak! Expect God to act!

Expect God to open the windows, and the doors of heaven and pour out a blessing unto you that you do not have room enough to receive! Expect your cup to run over! Expect to be overwhelmed, baptized in God's blessings! Expect the anointing! Expect to find the Father! Expect to find God! Expect to find the LORD! Expect God to reveal Himself unto you! Expect special delivery! God will deliver! Be in expectancy!

Do not let the devil fool you. Do not let the devil portray false imaginations in your mind. "Casting down **imaginations**, and every high thing that exalteth itself against the knowledge of God, and bringing into captivity every thought to the obedience of Christ." II Cor. 10:5. Do not let the devil steal your joy! The joy of the Lord is your strength.

Search, until you receive what you once had. Sometimes, the scenery will look as if what has been lost will never be found again; however, God said walk by faith and not by sight. You will receive it again. Keep cleaning. Keep your house clean.

One day as you are sweeping you will find what you have lost. You will find what you have longed for. You will find what you have missed. You will find what you have been dreaming of. You will find what people said could not be found! You will receive! You will say that this is the day that the Lord only has made, I will rejoice and be glad in it! God wants to give you an astounding testimony, so that others can overcome. You are an overcomer. Seek the Lord. You will find Him!

I found Him!
**He's on the inside of me!**
**He's everywhere!**
EUREKA!

*Worship is what Peter said to Jesus on the Mount of Transfiguration; "It is good for us to be here."*

*Worship is the x-ray into our spirits.*

*Worship is like mercury in a thermometer; it rises if it's hot; it falls if it's cold.*

# CHAPTER FIVE

# IN THE PRESENCE OF GOD

"Thou wilt shew me the path of life: in thy presence is fulness of joy; at thy right hand there are pleasures for evermore." Psalm 16:11

Here I am in the presence of God...alone...alone in His presence...alone with Him...alone with the Father. ...isolated...separated...detached....solo...apart from...face to face with Him...set apart...away from everything, and everyone, in a solitary place. There are no interruptions,  no distractions, or obstacles here to hinder me from communing  with my Father.  This is my secret place with the Father.

I begin to thank, praise, and then worship Him. I speak to Him in my heavenly language.  I sing songs unto Him.  I bow at His feet.

I lie prostrate before Him. I begin to weep. I am silent before Him. It's His awesome presence; it's His glory, His touch, His faithfulness, His deep love, His compassion, His warmth, His embrace, His peace, His gentleness, that hovers over me, and touches me. I'm alone in His presence.

I see Him sitting upon His throne, high and lifted up, His train fills all of heaven, and all of my temple within me. My body is the temple of God. He fills all of my spirit with His spirit. I am filled with the spirit of God. I am full! I am engulfed with His Spirit, His presence, His power, His love, and His joy. My heart is filled with His joy, with His warmth, with awe, with wonder, delight of His presence with me, and expectancy.

I feel the power of God anointing me. He's anointing my hands, my feet, my heart, my mind, and my thoughts. I sense Him overshadowing me, consuming me, lifting, encouraging, and inspiring me. My God is a consuming fire. He's searching my heart. He's dealing with past hurts, failures, pain, suffering, challenges, and past experiences. He's releasing me from them all. He ushers in forgiveness in my unforgivable situations.

Here I am, walking in the spirit, walking with God, talking with Him, bowing before Him. Here I am walking by faith, and not by sight. I am one with Him. We are one! His mind is my mind, his affections are my affections, His desires are my desires, His purposes are my purposes, His heart is my heart, His peace is my peace, which passeth all my understanding. We are one! Yes, we are one. Our desires are merging.....this is where my treasure is(Luke 12:34).....in Him.

I want more of Him. Lord, give me more,....more......more! I want to be with Him; I want to be in Him! Draw me closer! Draw me nearer. Bind me closer to you. Draw me into your bosom. Woo me into your presence. Hold me. Embrace me. Cuddle me. Touch me. Surround me. Draw me from within!

He must increase, I must decrease. John 3:30. Christ in me the hope of glory. Col. 1:27. I want more of His character in me. I want Him in control of me. I want Him to guide, lead, direct, and show me the way in which I must go. For He has said, "I am the way." John 14:6.

I asked Him to purge me with hyssop, that I might be whiter than snow. Forgive me. Cleanse me. Purge me. Wash me. Psalm 51.

I see Him taking a branch of hyssop plant. He's dipping it in Jesus' blood. Now I see Him, sprinkling the door posts of my heart, my mouth, my mind, my belly, my eyes, my ears, my hands, my feet; even my secret parts. He's purging me. He's washing me. He's cleansing me. He's flushing me. He's purging me with hyssop, that I might bow, and be holy in His presence. For I hear Him saying, "Worship me in the beauty of holiness!" Psa. 96:9.

I hear Him saying, "Come now, and let us reason together, saith the LORD: though your sins be as scarlet, they shall be as white as snow; though they be red like crimson, they shall be as wool(Isa. 1:18)....Take off your shoes from off thy feet, for the place whereon thou standest is holy ground(Ex. 3:5).....Be ye holy for I am holy."(I Pet. 1:16). We are one. We are holy. We are one in the Spirit. He has purged me with hyssop. I am whiter than snow. My sins are as wool. I am holy!

He begins to reveal to me His will, purpose, and destiny for my life. He unfolds, and unveils it before me. He is showing me a vision of His will. I see it, I bow down before Him, I understand more clearly.

I begin to share the hidden secrets of my heart with Him. He desires truth from the hidden parts of my heart. I share with Him, and bring to the table my weaknesses, shortcomings, mistakes, failures, pain, hurts, embarrassments, depressions, complexes, brokenness, and my misfortunes. He says, "My grace is more than sufficient for all these things." II Cor. 12:9. Be of good cheer, I have overcome the world. St. John 16:33.

In His presence, I wait to her His voice. My heart and ears long to wait to hear from Him! I long to hear His voice.

He begins to reveal Himself to me, in revelations, visions, and through His word. He says, "I am the way." John 14:6. I am your way. I am the bishop of your soul. I am your shepherd, and overseer. I am your King. I am your prince. You are mighty, for I am the Almighty! Go in peace my child! I love you!

*Worship is our means of walking on the water.*

*Worship is not falling short of the glory of God.*

*Worship is like starch; it takes the wrinkles out!*

# CHAPTER SIX

# THE PRACTICE OF THE PRESENCE OF GOD

**The Objective:** *To become aware of God's presence at all times. This is the essence of this section.*

As I enter the presence of God, and begin to develop a steadfast awareness of His presence, I found myself having to renounce everything that was unlike God. God is holy, and since God is holy, in order for me to dwell with Him, I must abandon, or surrender to anything, and everything that is unlike Him. Along with relinquishing unholy things in your life, you must drive away from your mind anything and everything that has power to interrupt or distract your thoughts of God.

Pay attention to your thoughts. If your thoughts are thinking on unholy things, then put those thoughts out of your mind; trample over them, blot them out, or cut them off. "Wherefore if thy hand or thy foot offend thee, cut them off, and cast [them] from thee: it is better for thee to enter into life halt or maimed, rather than having two hands or two feet to be cast into everlasting fire. And if thine **eye offend** thee, pluck it out, and cast [it] from thee: it is better for thee to enter into life with one eye, rather than having two eyes to be cast into hell fire." Matthew 18: 8, 9.

Faithfully, keep yourself in the presence of the Lord. "My son, attend to my words; incline thine ear unto my sayings. Let them not depart from thine eyes; keep them in the midst of thine heart. For they [are] life unto those that find them, and health **to all their flesh.**" Proverb 4:20-22. When I stay in God's presence, this hinders me from sinning against God, and it keeps me from doing that which might displease God.   When I stay in His presence, I begin to become familiar with Him; we become as one; our heartbeats, footsteps, ways, thoughts, and doings become as one.  God wants us to learn how to dwell in His presence.

As I abide in His presence, I know God more and more. When I walk with God, he begins to open up Himself to me more and more.  I am before God naked, and unashamed.  His presence become so natural to me that now, instead of thinking about going into His presence, I automatically go, without thought of me going, by becoming aware that He is here.

Give yourself totally to God, and resign from your patterns of sin, and your secret, hidden sins.  Give all of you to Him.  Sell out to Jesus.  Give up the sin and weights that so easily beset you.  Lose the weights.  **Lose weight!  You will be transformed!**

In the morning, think about Him; driving to work, think on Jesus.  On the job, in the midst of your business, think about Jesus; enter in His presence.  He is with you, and in you.  Your faith will increase the more you enter His presence.  Once your faith increase, you will begin to see drastic changes in your life.  You will begin to move mountains.  Things in your life that are broken, stuck, unmovable, unsolvable, unmanageable will be fixed.  Your unbelief will dwindle to nothing, your faith will increase.  Practice being in His presence.

The more you are in His presence, the greater God will make Himself known to you.  Your faith will increase.  "But without faith [it is] impossible to **please** [him]: for he that cometh to God must believe that he is, and [that] he is a rewarder of them that diligently seek him." Hebrews 11:6. God will reward you with what your faith is believing itself for. Fasting is another key.

Eventually, all of what you know of God will gradually become smaller. You will see different ways, thoughts, and characteristics of God which will be far greater than you ever imagined, or ever known of Him before. Your human ideas of God that you can conceive will no longer satisfy. God will be unworthy of these finite idioms, and conceptions that you once knew. God will awesomely reveal Himself to you in rare form. You will be changed. "Beloved, now are we the sons of God, and it doth not yet appear what we shall be: but we know that, when he shall appear, we shall be like him; for we shall see him as he is." I John 3:2. "And the Spirit of the LORD will come upon thee, and thou shalt prophesy with them, and shalt be turned into **another man**." I Samuel 10:6.

Persevere! Press! Push! Strive! Abide! Dwell! Seek! Search! Live in God's presence. Let nothing stop you. Meditate upon your strategy to continuously dwell, and be aware of His presence. PUSH! When the praises go up, His presence comes down! When the worship goes up, revelations come down!

He is full of grace and truth! Abandon yourself with Him. Cuddle yourself into His bosom. God will embrace you with His surrounding presence. He will open doors for you by His power. He will prepare the table before you, and commune with you. He will cause the heavens to open unto you.

I will gently rest in God. I will lay my head upon His bosom. There is an inexpressible sweetness that I taste and experience here. My desire is that God's countenance, and His glory show on my countenance, instead of my brokenness, wretchedness, hurt, pain, stress, discomfort, or any corruption.

Set time in your schedule for the Lord, and commune with Him. People may despise you for the time you share with Him. Sit in His presence as clay before the potter, as a stone before the carver. Let Him carve Himself into you. Let Him mold you, shape, fashion, design, change, transform, and make you. May you be like Him. Desire only Him. Give yourself to Him. Open up to Him. Be devoted to Him. Allow Him to take you to where He is.

*Worship produces life more abundantly.*

*The absence of the presence of the LORD*
*is like dry bones in a valley. Lifeless!*

*Worship is like taking a plunge into a pool of cool*
*water on a hot summer day. It refreshes you!*

# CHAPTER SEVEN

# TIMES OF REFRESHING

Repent ye therefore, and be converted, that your sins may be blotted out, **when the times of refreshing shall come from the presence of the Lord."** Acts 3:19.

**"Restore unto me the joy of thy salvation; and uphold me with thy free spirit."** Psalm 51:12.

### Refreshment

Need to be refreshed? Need a break? Need a vacation? A vacation spot? Looking for a resort area? Well, here's how you can be refreshed! **Your times of refreshment shall come from the presence of the Lord!**

The presence of the Lord is far greater than vacationing in London, Canada, the Bahamas, the Carribeans, the Hawaiian Islands, or the Virgin Islands. Where do you go to be refreshed? It's not the

Bahamas, but the presence of the Lord; it's not the Carribeans; but it's the presence of the Lord; it's not Atlantic City, but it's the presence of the Lord. The presence will bring refreshment to your soul, and my soul! How do I spell relief:

T-H-E  P-R-E-S-E-N-C-E  O-F  T-H-E  L-O-R-D!!!!!!!

In Acts 3:19, the word "times" is the Greek word "kairos," pronounced (kahee-ros'). It literally means a portion of time, or a season of time; it is God's timing; it's God's appointed time. The word "presence" is the Greek word "prosopon," pronounced (pros'-o-pon). It is defined as the face, or countenance of God. It is an outward appearance; a manifestation of oneself. So, it is in His time, *kairos time, appointed time,* that you receive refreshment to your soul.

The word refreshing is the Greek word "anapsuxis," pronounced (an-aps'-ook-sis). It is defined as a cooling restoration. Refreshing is to impart renewed energy, power, peace, or strength to; to rejuvenate. Refreshing also means to revive or to be refreshed with rest, food, drink, or the presence of the Lord. To be refreshed is to give a new brightness to or to give new added vigor to. When you are refreshed, you are made cool, or clean; you freshen up. Refreshment causes you to be filled up, or rejuvenated again. When you are refreshed, you are whole, or complete again from a new supply. You become inspired, and nourished. When you are refreshed, you are made new again. You've been renovated, refurbished, or reconditioned. You are fresh, alive, and different. Let the word of God revive you again! For the word of God is quick, and powerful! Quick means that it makes alive!

The presence of the Lord is the key source of your refreshment. The presence of the Lord serves as an instructor to reacquaint you with material, strength, life, wholeness, power, anointing, and might in which you previously possessed. The presence of the Lord operates in light of bringing your strength, knowledge or skills back up to date.

In this verse, repentance will bring "seasons of refreshing from the presence of the Lord." Your heart will be restored, your mind will be renewed, your strength will be revigorated, and your spirit will be refreshed and strong once again.

Come unto God's presence; there is healing there. There is victory, deliverance, freedom, restoration, life, insight, wholeness, prosperity, wealth, favor, benefits, visions, dreams, revelations, intimacy, purpose, destiny, and all that you need. **God not only wants you to come into His presence; but He wants you to dwell in His presence.**

### Restoration

"Restore unto me the joy of thy salvation; and uphold me with thy free spirit." Psa. 51:12. To restore is the Hebrew word "shuwb," pronounced (shoob). It means to return, or to turn back. Restore in this verse means to turn back to God, or to repent. Restoration involves turning from evil, wickedness, and every false way. Restoration goes into a more deeper definition than to be refreshed, or to be repaired. Restoration is a leading away from an obstacle. It brings you back to where you detoured. To restore is to cause the thing that hindered you to become defeated, refused, or rejected. You turn against the thing that has kept you down, and turn towards God. To restore is to be brought back, reversing or revoking the evil that hindered you. David asked the Lord to restore the joy of His salvation.

In other passages of scripture, there are cries made unto the Lord for restoration.

"Turn us again, O God of Hosts, and cause thy face to shine; and we shall be saved." Psa. 80:7.

"For I will restore health unto thee, and I will heal thee of thy wounds, saith the LORD; because they called thee an Outcast, saying, This is Zion, whom no man seeketh after." Jer. 30:17.

"Turn thou us unto thee, O LORD, and we shall be turned; renew our days as of old." Lam. 5:21.

"I will restore to you the years that the locust hath eaten, the cankerworm, and the caterpillar, and the palmerworm, my great army which I sent among you." Joel 2:25.

"The Lord is my shepherd; I shall not want. He maketh me to lie down in green pastures: he leadeth me beside the still waters. He restoreth my soul: he leadeth me in the paths of righteousness for his name's sake. Yea, though I walk through the valley of the shadow of death, I will fear no evil: for thou art with me; thy rod and thy staff they comfort me." Psalm 23:1-4.

From this Psalm, David is restored in the presence of the Lord. Verse 4 states.... "for thou art with me." If the Lord is with you, and in you, then you are in His presence. The Lord leadeth you by the still, quiet, soothing waters, and then restoreth your soul. The word 'still' is the Hebrew word "menuwchah," pronounced (men-oo-khaw'). It means a resting place; **a quiet place of rest.**

God is with you; His rod and staff shall comfort you. The word comfort means to have compassion on. It means to console, or to bring about ease. This is the word "nacham," pronounced (naw-kham'). Stay with the Lord in His presence, and He shall restore, refresh, and comfort you. Dwell in the presence of the Lord forever. Oh, taste and see that it is good, good, good!

Take a plunge into God's presence!<br>Be thou refreshed!

**Worship God in the Beauty of Holiness!**

*Worship is like yeast baking in bread, you cannot
ascend or rise unto God without it.*

*Worship without ceasing.*

*Worship is our textbook to knowing God.*

# CHAPTER EIGHT

# THE DESIRE TO KNOW HIM

"That I may know him, and the power of his resurrection, and
the fellowship of his sufferings, being made conformable unto his
death; If by any means I might attain unto the resurrection of the
dead." Philippians 3:10.

I want to know God! I want to know Him! There are
many things I know about God. When I became a born again Christian, I began to learn of God. Some of His characteristics that I learned
of Him were that He was meek, lowly in heart, and a place of rest for
me. Matthew 11:29. To learn of God is to increase one's knowledge of
Him. To learn of Jesus is to hear; and to be informed. This word learn
is the Greek word, "manthano," pronounced (man-than'-o). It is to

learn of Him by use and practice. That's why it is said to practice the presence of God. You practice His presence by being in the habit of coming into His presence, and becoming accustomed, or aware of Him. As I continue my practice, habit, and become accustomed, and aware of God's presence, I learn of Him, and begin to know Him more and more.

My desire is to know Him. There are many things in life that I can pursue; however, my pursuit of God is my highest desire, dream, longing, and my greatest passion. I desire to know God. Above the ministry, above that job, above that person, above that greatest desire is a longing within my heart, and within my spirit to know, and love Him.

As I look over the congregation, I see many people that I am acquainted with from the past. For many of them, I only know their names, some I know by face only, some I know by what they do in ministry, and others I know by where they work. On the other hand, there are some who I know of their likes, their dislikes, their favorite expressions, their background, their skills, talents, gifts, their birthplace, parents, children, and marital status. With these people I know what angers them, what breaks their hearts, what makes them sad, happy, or ecstatic. In other words, I know them! I know them intimately!

**When I know a person intimately, I know how to please them.** On the contrary, **I know what displeases them. My desire is to be pleasing, and to please.** My desire is to know God, and to please Him. "But **without faith** [it is] impossible to please [him]: for he that cometh to God must first believe that he is, and [that] he is a rewarder of them that diligently seek him." Hebrews 11:6.

To please God is to bring Him enjoyment, pleasure, or satisfaction; to make Him glad or contented. **To know Him is to please Him.** When I please God I am in His will. This is God's desire, and will, for me to please Him. When I please God, I am agreeable, and one with Him. He is delighted, and satisfied with my actions.

God is pleased when I walk in the spirit. Romans 8:8 states, "So then they that are in the flesh cannot please God." I must please God. I must seek to know Him. As spouses seek to know each other, so must we seek to know Christ.

Jeremiah 29:13 says, "And ye shall **seek me, and find [me]**, when ye shall search for **me** with **all your heart.** To seek is the Hebrew word "baqash," pronounced (baw-kash'). It means to seek with intentions on finding; desire, or request. To seek also is defined as to seek to secure, to seek the face or the presence, to demand or to ask. We seek God, to find Him, to enquire of Him, and to know Him. We need to find out where God is, and then seek Him there. He said to seek Him where He may be found. He does not intend for us to seek Him where we want Him to be, but where He is. He is on the inside of you. God is everywhere!

Paul's greatest quest was to know Jesus. In Philippians 3:10, to know is the Greek word, "ginosko," pronounced (ghin-oce'-ko). It means to learn or to know, to come to know, to get and have knowledge of; to perceive, or to feel. Ginosko also is defined as becoming acquainted with; or to know in terms of sexual intercourse between a man and a woman.

My knowledge of Jesus should be more than head knowledge of Him, but knowledge from my personal, close encounters, and experiences. My knowledge of Him is obtained by my proximity to Him, that is, my closeness, and my understanding of Him

My goal is to also know Him through insight, and through knowledge gained through my senses. Oh, to see Him, to feel His touch, to hear his voice, to feel His presence, to sense His presence, and to taste Him. Psalm 34:8 says, "O taste and see that the LORD is good: blessed is the man that trusteth in Him."

Isaiah said, "In the year that king Uzziah died I saw also the Lord sitting upon a throne, high and lifted up, and his train filled the temple." Isaiah 6:1. The word "saw" is the Hebrew word "ra'ah," pronounced (raw-aw'). It means to see, to look at, to inspect, perceive, or to consider. Raah also means to see by having a vision; to discern, distinguish, or to gaze at. I want to know Him!

Our power in our relationship with Jesus lies in deeply knowing Him. Paul desired to know Jesus in three ways: in the power of his resurrection, in the fellowship of his sufferings, and to be made conformable unto his death. When we know Jesus in the fullest extent of knowledge, this means that we now know Him in the power of His resurrection, in the fellowship of His sufferings, and we have been made conformable unto His death. All three of these ingredients express the highest expression of Jesus' mission. We must suffer with Him, as well as reign with Him, and to produce His glory. I long to know Him in all of His fullness! It produces life within me! Know God.

**No God; No reign!**
**Know God; Know reign!**
**Know Him!**

*Worship is like counting numbers, the higher you count, or go, the higher the value; the lower you count, or go, the lower the value.*

*Worship is like a lighted, fragrance candle. The more the fire burns; the more the sweet smelling aroma-savor ascends into the heavens.*

*Like entering the beauty salon to make you beautiful, so is entering worship. It beautifies you!*

# CHAPTER NINE

# SITTING BEFORE THE LORD

"Then went King David in, and **sat before the Lord**, and he said, Who am I, O Lord GOD; and what is my house, that thou hast brought me hitherto?" II Samuel 7:18.

"O how love I thy law! It is **my meditation** all the day. Thou through thy commandments hast made me wiser than it has made mine enemies: for they are ever with me. I have more understanding than all my teachers: for thy testimonies are my meditation. I understand more than the ancients, because I keep thy precepts." Psalm 119:97-100.

"This book of the law shall not depart out of thy mouth; but thou shalt **meditate therein day and night**, that thou mayest observe to do according to all that is written therein: for then thou shalt make thy way prosperous, and then thou shalt have good success." Joshua 1:8.

Notice the phrase, '**sat before the Lord**' in II Samuel 7:18, "Then went king David in, and sat before the Lord, and he said, Who am I, O Lord GOD; and what is my house, that thou hast brought me hitherto?" Although the phrase states that David sat before the Lord, he was not just sitting in a chair as we know it; the connotation has a deeper meaning hidden within. The phrase literally means that David was kneeling, listening, talking, and meditating upon the Lord.

The word 'sat' is the Hebrew word 'yashab,' pronounced (yawshab'). It means to dwell, remain, abide, to take one's abode, inhabit, tarry, continue, or to cause to sit. Another astounding definition of 'sat' is to remain in a place to the extent that you become as one and are deeply connected to that person, and is expressed in terms of being married.

The word 'before,' in II Samuel 7:18, is the Hebrew word 'paniym,' pronounced (paw-neem'). Surprisingly, it is the same word used for 'the face of God', which is expressed as the presence of God. 'Before' means: face, presence, before and behind, toward, in front of, forward, in the presence of, in the face of, at the face or in the sight of. Now this definition is interesting, isn't it?

Now, we are not to think that David was sitting at ease in a lounge chair, or lazy boy. Research shows that he was upon the ground, as one would do in Oriental customs, with his feet doubled, and folded under him, with his head bow forward in humility. This type of sitting posture was a position of meditation. In this position, David poured out his thoughts before God. This position spoke of adoration, reverence, lowliness, and deep humility before the Lord. The lowly posture spoke of David's lowly, humble state of mind before God. It was also a symbol of the veiled presence before Him. Humility is the first step on the ladder whose top or peak reaches heaven. There you will find the presence of God, the voice of God, the purpose and heart of God.

David sat before the Lord pouring out his thoughts, feelings, concerns, and worshiped God. David began to meditate, and to speak to God. Meditating on God is an activity of thinking over things, dwelling on, contemplating, and applying yourself to the thoughts about the works, ways, purposes, visions, directions, or promises of God. Your thoughts are holy towards God. God helps you to commune with Him. We meditate upon God to clear our mental and spiritual vision of Him, and allow Him to direct our thoughts toward the truth. The effects of meditating is to humble us as we think on God's greatness, infiniteness, power and glory. As we think on these things, we begin to think of our finiteness, weakness, and sinfulness. The meditation ultimately encourages us, and lifts us up to not think about ourselves in our perspective, but what God thinks, and says about us. He reassures us, strengthens us, and shows us His paths and destiny for our lives. We must make meditation, and sitting before the Lord a priority in our lives.

Some of the benefits of sitting before the Lord and meditating upon Him are found in the following passages of scripture. Review them carefully. Search for other benefits in the Word of God. "O how love I thy law! It is my meditation all the day. Thou through thy commandments hast made me wiser than it has made mine enemies: for they are ever with me. I have more understanding than all my teachers: for thy testimonies are my meditation. I understand more than the ancients, because I keep thy precepts." Psalm 119:97-100. Selah.

"This book of the law shall not depart out of thy mouth; but thou shalt meditate therein day and night, that thou mayest observe to do according to all that is written therein: for then thou shalt make thy way prosperous, and then thou shalt have good success." Joshua 1:8. Selah. What excellent benefits! Just to mention a few of the benefits of meditating: you become wiser than your enemies, wiser with more understanding than your teachers. Your understanding will be more than many of old. Your wisdom will increase. You will become keener with greater, sharper insight; sharper discernment, and heightened obedience. Your way will be prosperous, and **YOU WILL HAVE GOOD SUCCESS!**

**Meditation is God's way of rewarding our lives with His success and prosperity.** It is not following a lot of prosperity plans, or following the keys to success that the world has prescribed, but these things are obtained by you staying before the Lord in His presence.

The word 'prosperous,' in Joshua 1:8, is the Hebrew word 'tsalach,' pronounced (tsaw-lakh'). Prosperous means that you will advance, make great progress, succeed, and are profitable. You will become mighty! You must obey this verse of scripture in order to be prosperous!

The word 'success,' in Joshua 1:8, is the Hebrew word 'sakal,' pronounced (saw-kal'). It means that you will be prudent. You will wisely understand things, and you will prosper. It further means that you will have great, rich, insight and comprehension. You will possess extraordinary skills.

Success, health, riches, honor, prosperity, life, wisdom, discernment, insight, skills, favor, and greatness are found in God's presence. I need to go there, and stay there! "...For your life is hid with Christ in God." Colossians 3:3. Meditate upon God's word, and on Him. Stay before God. Bow before Him; worship Him at His feet. Ponder His ways and His works. Sit before the Lord.

We pray that whatever hinders you from sitting and dwelling before the Lord, will suddenly cease its existence in your life. We pray that life will flow in its abundance to you in sitting before the Lord. In the name of Jesus, you will no longer use all of your time thinking about, or meditating on: ungodly imaginations, the lusts of your flesh, and the lusts of your eye. You will have wholesome, holy, righteous thoughts; and they will be turned, and tuned towards God. You will obey God, even in thinking righteous thoughts.

In Jesus name, you will prioritize your schedule to sit before the Lord in His presence—not two or three times per week, but every single day. For this to be effective, you must do it daily. Watch your life begin to change and soar to new grounds, new hopes, new visions, new dreams, and new dimensions unknown to you. God will do the impossible. God will do the things that you know not of! You will no longer sit before HBO, but before the Lord. You will not sit thinking of unclean thoughts, but you will begin to think more on Jesus, and who He is. If you can sit watching television most of the day, you can reverse that habit, and instead sit before God, in the mighty name of Jesus.

You will reap, if you faint not. Try it; you'll like it! As you continually tell God, "Not my will, but thine be done," God will begin to manifest, and heal those experiences that are lingering in your heart that hurt and break you. These are wounds that you generally do not think of day to day, but when the thought of it comes to your mind, or when you are confronted with that hurt, you are crushed with deep hurt and/or pain by that wound. Come into God's presence, that inner healing can take place. God wants to set you free from inner scars of the past.

Come into God's presence; sit before Him. He will automatically begin to do all sorts of things to make you better. The hidden hurts in your heart that no one knows about but God is what God is coming after to bring deliverance.

Allow God to pour His ointment, His Anointing power, and His sweet soft healing love into your heart and into your inner hidden pain.

"Is there no balm in Gilead; is there no physician there? Why then is not the health of the daughter of my people recovered?" Jer. 8:22. *Balm* in this verse is a type of aromatic resin exuded, oozed, or seeped from the plant, 'Balm of Gilead.' It is salve from a tree, which is an analgesic, or medicinal ointment that soothes, or heals. Balm is a type of balsam. Balsam is a fragrant ointment taken from a tree, used as medication.

In this verse of scripture, the Balm of Gilead is symbolic of Jesus Christ, who is Jehovah Rapha, The God that healeth thee. Surrender your pain, and deep hurt to the Father that He might pour in the fragrant anointing ointment into your life. You will be healed of your wounds! "Heal me, O LORD, and I shall be healed; save me, and I shall be saved: for thou art my praise." Jer. 17:14. The word heal is the Hebrew word 'rapha.' It means to make healthy, cure, repair, or to heal.

## The Effects of Sitting before the Lord

Many things transpire, or happen behind the scenes, as we sit before the Lord. Primarily, as we sit before the Lord, there is an exclusion of the world and it influences on us. The more and more each day you spend in the presence of the Lord, the less and less the world's opinions, pleasures, devices, influences, or attachments, will vanish from your view. Everything becomes as shadows, and become dim, in the light of the presence of God. The greater your time is with the Lord in His presence, the more the world appears as nothing to you. God gradually delivers you from the blinding and perverting influence that the world may has upon you.

You cannot keep sitting before God, and not be changed! "But we all, with open face beholding as in a glass the glory of the Lord, are changed into the same image from glory to glory, even as by the Spirit of the Lord." II Cor. 3:18.

The open face is an unveiled face. The more I behold, and reflect the glory of God, the greater the transformation. The word changed in this verse is the Greek word 'metamorphoo,' pronounced (met-am-or-fo'-o). This word is where we get our English word metamorphosis. The word means to change into another form; to transform by power; or to transfigure. This transformation, or transfiguration is permanent. It displays a marked change in appearance, character, condition, or function.

Secondly, when we sit before the Lord, it begins to create an intense consciousness of God. The Lord's character, and works, will begin to stand forth more glorious and impressive.

Thirdly, when we sit before God, it begins to create a more intense consciousness of ourselves, our real nature, our relationships, and our responsibilities to God and man. In other words, in the presence of God, He will begin to reveal to us who we really are. Light exposes all things. All things are naked before the Lord.

"Neither is there any creature that is not manifest in his sight: but all things are naked and opened unto the eyes of him with whom we have to do." Heb. 4:13.

Expect personal revelation of who you are. Expect parts of you that you did not even know that existed within you to come to surface. There is nothing hidden that shall not be revealed. In II Samuel 7:18, "...as David sat before the Lord, he asked.... **Who am I, O Lord GOD?**"

Fourthly, when you sit in the presence of God, it will develop a greater susceptibility to God's divine influences, and receptivity of his divine gifts. When you ask for more of Him, that is what you will receive. Prepare your heart to receive more of the Holy Spirit; and you will definitely receive more.

## Spiritual Profits of Sitting before the Lord

In sitting before the Lord, you receive a fuller, deeper, and truer knowledge of insight into His nature, and character. We will begin to understand better, his plans, methods, will, purposes, and destiny for our lives. Our thoughts of God will begin to enlarge, and to quicken. We will become tuned in to God's heart. **Our passion for His presence will bring forth compassion for one another.**

Another benefit or profit from meditating upon the Lord is that it creates deeper, richer, higher emotions and affections within us. Humility, gratitude, love, confidence, hope, peace, joy, and patience are nourished best in the presence of the Lord. As we come in His presence perpetually, pronouncing our failures, sins, mistakes, faults, and weaknesses, we will receive a greater, more hopeful outlook and perspective resolution. As we bring our fears to the throne, we will be relieved of them and He will cause us to gain new courage, new visions, new hopes, new dreams, new outlooks, new focuses, inner healing, and patience in our everyday circumstances and situations. Come unto Him. Let Him instruct us. Let Him console, and comfort us.

Another benefit in sitting before the Lord is that we will begin to produce, and present better worship unto the Lord. Because of the richness, and wealth of abundance that God presents to us as we sit before Him, divine worship will naturally spring forth. Worship that is not offered before the Lord is not worship.

Finally, sitting before the Lord will produce a greater power for me live up to the convictions and to the law of the Lord. We grow stronger, wiser, bolder, braver, more loving, and more compassionate from glory to glory to glory as we stay in His presence. We endure hardness as good soldiers, because of the anointed power flowing in our lives. We will begin to do exploits. Signs and wonders will follow us. We will lay our hands on the sick and they shall recover. We will flow in the wisdom of God. We will stand in the power and knowledge of God. Devils and demons will obey us.

If we do not sit before the Lord, we forfeit our highest joy, highest happiness, highest blessings, highest potential, highest ability, highest destiny, highest gain, greatest abundance, and our highest and richest wealth. **Do not neglect sitting before the Lord.** It's your highest source of resource. **It's my utmost, for His highest!**

### Principle Thoughts of Meditation before the Lord

In sitting before the Lord, review your past, present, and future. This is an excellent way to begin your moments of meditation with Him. As you review them, notice the pattern of God's work being performed in your life. Remember the battles God won for you, and the many victories He wrought in your life. Remember the miracles, deliverances, healings, and the mighty harvest He brought forth in your life, and begin to thank Him.

In all of your dealings, notice the holy hand of God in the midst of it all. Think of all of the mercy and grace that God is pouring into your life. After thinking on these things now you will be able to better distinguish, and anticipate God's movement in your present situations, and you will be able to prophetically discern His movements for your future.

Another principle is for you to reflect upon God. Reflect upon His awesome greatness, His goodness, His mercy, His grace, and His mighty power. Reflect upon the supernatural character of God. Begin to honor and worship Him. Extol Him above all things.

Focus on His Word. The more we reflect and focus on the greatness of God, the smaller and smaller our problems become. Our problems, sicknesses, diseases, illnesses, burdens, scars, wounds, hurts, failures, and fears shrink in His presence. Once we compare them with God's greatness, then they are only shadows before Him. They shrink to nothing, because God is far greater in might, strength, and power. The more I focus on my problems, the greater I become overwhelmed with the problem. The more I focus on God, the more I will become overwhelmed with Him, and the more those overcoming problems move into their perspective, and proper places. Things will no longer overwhelm, and discourage you.

Another principle is to reflect upon the promises of God. In the Word, God promises many things. These promises increase our faith, and our burdens will begin to decrease. Allow God's immediate presence to calm your every care.

The last principle is to make a request of the Father. Now you can ask, and you shall receive; you will seek, and you shall find; and you will knock, and the door will open unto you. Matt. 7:7. "Call unto me, and I will answer thee, and shew thee the great and the mighty things, which thou knowest not." Jer. 33:3.

### Prerequisites for Sitting before the Lord

### Seclusion

One of the first things that must be incorporated in your time in sitting before the Lord, is seclusion. Seclusion is setting, and keeping apart from social contact with others. Seclusion is making your time with the Lord a private affair. You must isolate yourself from the rest of the world to totally focus on God. Separate yourself from the busy activities that you normally engage in each day. Turn off telephones, televisions, radios, videos, computers, or any distracting thing.

Notice Mark 1:35: "Now in the morning, having risen a long while before daylight, He went out and departed to a solitary place; and there He prayed." The word 'solitary,' is the Greek word 'eremos,' pronounced (er'-ay-mos). The word means desolate, lonely, and uninhabited. It is a state of being deserted by others; deprived of any aid and protection of others, especially of close friends, acquaintances, or kindred.

Some of us are so attached to others that it would be extremely difficult for them to disconnect, and detach themselves from you. If Jesus separated Himself and went to a secluded place, then it is definitely, and extremely important for us to separate ourselves, too. Everyone needs to be alone sometimes. God wants your undivided attention as you sit before Him. God wants YOU! Get alone with God.

### Alone or Lonely?

When we separate ourselves sitting before God, we are alone, and not lonely! Are you alone, or lonely? When I am lonely, my thoughts are on me. I may feel sorry for myself, or I may have feelings of being dejected due to the awareness of being alone, or just being lonely. When you are lonely, you are without companions; you are desolate. You feel deserted! Your focus is in the wrong place. Your focus is on yourself, and the fact that you are alone. This feeling produces dejection with you.

When you however are alone, you do not necessarily feel lonely. To be alone is being apart from others in a solitary place. You are without others, without help or aid. Being alone only means that you are isolated from others. To be alone is to aid one in focusing in on the Lord wholeheartedly. To be alone helps you to better focus, and target in on the Lord, and worship Him without any hindrances, delays, distractions, obstacles, aggravations, or barriers. Are you alone or lonely?

### Silence, Quietness
"In quiet and confidence shall be your strength." Isaiah 30:15. The word quiet in this verse is the Hebrew word 'shaqat,' pronounced (shaw-kat'). It means to be in a quiet and peaceful place. This place is further defined as a place where you are undisturbed, or inactive. It also means to be in a state of rest, or to be in a state of relief. This is a place where the war has ended, the fighting has ceased, the violence is over, and now peace is established.

God wants us to sometimes approach His presence in quietness. We pray to God; however, prayer is defined as talking to God. God wants to talk, and commune with us. Which is better, for us to talk to God, or for God to speak to us? How are we going to hear God, and we always have our mouths opened addressing Him?

God wants the quietness and silence, so He can speak. Let God get in some words sometimes. Sit quietly before the Lord. Take a note pad, and a pencil. Write what God says. Review and obey His statements. Listen attentively. Wait for His voice to speak unto your heart. Wait for Him!

When I enter the presence of God, I long to hear His voice! I long to sense His presence, His touch, His hug, His breath, His kiss, His embrace, His presence encompassing me. As I think of His might, His greatness, His brilliance, His majesty, His power, His presence, I sit in awe of who He is. I bow before His majesty. His majesty is depicted through His title of King in that when He speaks, everything obeys His command. Things fall, things stop, things open, things close, things grow, things dissolve, things die, things multiply, things bow, things shut up, things break, things shatter, things flee, things are destroyed, things are healed, things are promoted, things obey, things surrender, things are blessed or cursed, things are created, things bring life, things are empowered, things are freed, or things are loosed or bound!

Whatever He commands, obedience follows, for He is God and God alone. There is none like Him. He said that there are no other gods beside Him. When kings stretch out their scepter, and command, obedience follows. Likewise, unto the King of All the heavens, and the earth. This demonstrates God's majesty!

### Stillness

"Be still, and know that I am God." Psa. 46:10. The word 'still' is the Hebrew word 'raphah,' pronounced (raw-faw'). This word is pronounced like the Hebrew word for healing (rapha). It means to relax, withdraw, abandon, to be quiet, **to be idle**, or to cease. I love the part of the definition to be idle. To be idle is to not be employed, or busy. It also means to be lazy. In this case, we are not talking about the definition of being lazy, but of not being active.

When I was younger, I would hear other people say not to be idle, because it was the devil's workshop. I beg to differ with this statement. To be idle is to be still. You can be still and allow the devil to entertain your thoughts, or you can allow the Holy Spirit to actively speak to you in your state of being still. In your state of idleness, shame the devil, and give God the glory. Evict the devil and his workshop, and open up a new holy avenue of thoughts in God's workshop! Get idle for God!

Stillness promotes concentration. Become and pray for sensitivity. Be sensitive to the voice of God, and His presence. Be sensitive before Him. Stop your mind from wandering. Concentrate. When we become still, everything else is driven away.

### Submission, Humility

"Humble yourselves in the sight of the Lord, and He will lift you up." Jms. 4:10. Come before God's presence with singing. Enter into His gates with thanksgiving, and into His courts with praise.... Bless His name. Psa. 100.

Surrender to God's will, way, plan, and purpose for your life. Remember that your provision, blessings, life, healings, honor, strength, wealth, and your abundance are found in you being in God's will. Your provision is found in being in the will of God. Sometimes, we do not have because we are outside of God's will. My utmost for His highest!

My utmost is my surrender, humility, and obedience to the Lord. When I surrender all things to God, then I no longer declare any ownership, or control of any of those things. Rebellion is opposed to obedience. Jesus Christ humbled himself and became obedient even to the death of the cross. Phil. 2:8. That is why God highly exalted Him. Yield to the will of God.

Deal with the problems, scars, dysfunctional emotions, embarrassments, hurts, abuse, poverty, rejection, or weaknesses in the way in which God directs you. He will lead you to health, victory, deliverance, miracles, and to reaping a harvest beyond your imagination!

Sit before God; that's where your healing is found! Sit before God; that's where your solutions and answers are found! Sit before God; that's where your victory lies! Sit before God; that's where your peace is found! You will reap a harvest!

Expect to receive recovery! Expect to receive a cure! Expect your healing! Look for the unexpected miracle! Expect to receive promotion! Expect to be wiser! Expect to have power over your flesh! Expect to be stronger! Expect to achieve, and overcome what always was a hindrance to you! Expect to receive power to daily come into God's presence! Expect God's presence to be so real to you! Expect God to lead you in every situation in your life! Expect life! Expect life more abundantly!

Leave everything to God. Take your hands off of situations. Act as if you are dumb to what should be done in your dilemma. Leave everything to God. "Be still and know that I am God." Psalm 46:10. He will handle things, if you surrender it to Him!

Do you want, or need attention? Come into God's presence! He's always there to send an influx of His might, love, life, and power to His worshipers.

*Worship is like flying a kite, the more wind*
*(Spirit) you have, the higher you will go.*

*Preparation for the Olympics is similar to worship.*
*It must be done each day for success.*

*Worship God in spirit and in truth, not in flesh and in truth.*

# CHAPTER TEN

# BONDING WITH GOD

**"Abide in me, and I in you."** St. John 15:4.
"....And truly our fellowship is with the Father, and with his Son Jesus Christ." I John 1:3.
"And thou shalt love the Lord thy God with all thy heart, and with all thy soul, and with all thy mind, and with all thy strength: this is the first commandment." Mark 12:30.
"Nevertheless, I have somewhat against thee, because thou hast left thy first love." Revelation 2:4.

### The Parent-Infant Bond
Parents and babies naturally form a strong relationship, and bond with each other. The parent-infant bond is the common terminology used in developing a strong relationship among the parent, and

their new baby. For the parent, the bond is formed through love, and
responsibility to the child. For the infant, this is their first, and most
important relationship. This is their first love!

Remember, God said in Revelation 2:4 to the church of Ephesus,
"Nevertheless I have somewhat against thee, because thou hast left thy
first love." "We love him, because he first loved us." I John 4:19.

For the infant, this first love relationship is drastically important.
This relationship sets the tone, and stage for all later interpersonal relationships in the infant's life.

It has been researched that if the parent-infant bond does not develop, then in future relationships, the child will not be able to love as
an adult in a wholesome way. The relationship between the infant and
parent actually teaches the child how to love men and women in their
later seasons. The boys learn how to love men and women, and vice
versa with the girls.

Without the bond between the infant and their parents, it is pos-
sible that not only will the child have problems in developing long
lasting relationships, but may drift into homosexual, or lesbian relationships in the future. The parents, at the child's infant stage, are
actually teaching the child how to love the right way.

The parent-infant bond has several activities which help to formulate a strong tie. These activities may include parents being sensitive,
and responsive to the infant. The parenting must be consistent. Parents must love, feed, nurture, handle, cuddle, hold, smile, laugh, share,
change, wash, dress, console, comfort, play, talk with, care for, and
pray over their infants in order for the bonding to occur. The kissing,
the cuddling, the holding, the hugging, and the touching bring you
closer together within the bond, or tie. Without it, there will not be a
strong bond between the parent and their infant.

The infants must not be left alone. They depend upon you to
provide everything for them. Infants are highly emotional beings, and
very sensitive. You must provide food, shelter, and clothing for the
infant; however, the infant longs for your affection above all.

Infants are blank pages; they are empty vessels. You must teach
them how to love. You teach them how to love by pouring love into
them. Eventually, the infants will begin to reciprocate gestures, emotions, and affections back to you. They will respond to your respon-
siveness to them. Pour love into their hearts, warmth, and affection.
Impart unto them. Pour into them.

### The God-Worshipper Bond

"....And truly our fellowship is with the Father, and with his Son Jesus Christ." I John 1:3. "And thou shalt love the Lord thy God with all thy heart, and with all thy soul, and with all thy mind, and with all thy strength: this is the first commandment." Mark 12:30. "Nevertheless, I have somewhat against thee, because thou hast left thy first love." Revelation 2:4. "Abide in me, and I in you." St. John 15:4.

To bond with God means that we become bound, fastened, and tied to Him. I'm addicted to Jesus. We are linked to Him. As Paul was a prisoner of the Lord Jesus, so are His worshipers. We are prisoners of the Lord, not by force, but because we love God so much. We love God with all our heart, mind, soul, and strength. We worship Him by standing in awe of Him.

The bond with God is a union or cohesion brought about by love. As we first became Christians, Jesus was our first love. We love Him because He first loved us.

We bond with God by abiding with Him. "Abide in me, and I in you." St. John 15:4.

Parents bond with their children by spending time with them cuddling them, holding them, consoling them, etc, so likewise, God's presence surrounds me, holds me, cuddles me, and consoles me. The more and more I spend time with God, the stronger the bond will be between us. God says that He will never leave you, nor forsake you. He is always with us. It is imperative that you become aware of God's presence at all times. When you are a prisoner, you are bound, and are a captive. We are not captives by force, but because we love God so much, we are tied, and bound to Him. We cannot do anything without Him. We cannot even move without Him. Read Acts 17:28.

God desires to fellowship with you, and to bond with you. Stay connected to him. Abide in the vine. Be the branches of the vine, that abides, clings, and climbs unto Him. Cling to him. Abide in Him. Yoke with Him.

Become one with the Father. Love up on the Father. Embrace His love. Receive His love. Bond with God.

*Worship is tangible anointing.*

*Worship is like riding a bicycle. It keeps you balanced!*

*Like logs floating on the water, so worship causes you to float above situations, sickness, diseases, circumstances, and any problem!*

# CHAPTER ELEVEN

# PLAYING BEFORE GOD

" **A**nd it came to pass, [as] the ark of the covenant of the LORD came to the city of David, that Michal the daughter of Saul looking out at a window saw **king David dancing and playing**: and she despised him in her heart." I Chronicles 15:29.

"And **David and all the house of Israel played before the LORD** on all manner of instruments made of fir wood, even on harps, and on psalteries, and on timbrels, and on cornets, and on cymbals." II Samuel 6:5.

And David said unto Michal, "It was before the LORD, which chose me before thy father, and before all his house, to appoint me ruler over the people of the LORD, over Israel: therefore will **I play before the LORD**." II Samuel 6:21.

"And **David and all Israel played before God** with all their might, and with singing, and with harps, and with psalteries, and with timbrels, and with cymbals, and with trumpets." I Chronicles 13:8.

As parents watch their children play before them, it brings them joy. It brings them joy knowing that their children are happy. The children are worry-free! The children are stress-free!

In I Chronicles 15:29, King David was dancing and playing before the LORD. The word "playing" is the Hebrew word "sachaq." pronounced (saw-khak'). This word is the same word used for laughing. Sachaq means to laugh, play, jest, mock, and to sport. This word also means to play which includes instrumental music, singing, and dancing.

   To play means to occupy oneself in amusement, delight, or sport; or to toy. It also means to behave or converse in a sportive, or playful way. To play means to move or seem to move quickly, lightly, or irregularly; without any organized, rehearsed, or practiced patterns. The word also carries the meaning of moving, or operating freely within a bounded or unbounded space. There is ease of movement; freedom, and swing that demonstrates joy. Therefore, you are free, at liberty, unlimited, and boundless in your actions. Nothing is formatted or planned. There is no set organization to playing. It is spontaneously done! It happens without an agenda, or program. You are free in your movements! Free for you to move according to the Spirit of God. There is a lot to learn from this word.

   God wants us to play before Him. Be free and at liberty. God wants you to play with no set pattern, plan, outline, or agenda; but, just simply come as children before Him. Play before God.

   God is calling His people to move freely before Him. God is calling His body to move in the spirit before Him, quickly, lightly, with irregular, spontaneous movements! God is calling His people to be filled with laughter, delight, gladness, and with great joy! God is calling His royal priesthood, His chosen nation of people to move and operate in the Spirit in an unlimited space with great delight and joy! Let go of the boundaries! Release your program, and your agenda. God wants His nation of people to play before Him.

When you play, you are not troubled, worried, stressed, or deeply concerned about anything. When we play before God, it depicts that we are trouble-free, worried-free, and stress-free. Our trust is in the LORD. We believe that God is in control. As we behold God in His glory, we are confident that God is fighting our battles, and causing us to prosper in every way.

Psalm 37:4,5 says "Delight thyself also in the LORD: and he shall give thee the desires of thine heart. Commit thy way unto the LORD; trust also in Him; and he shall bring it to pass." Delight is the Hebrew word "`anag" pronounced (aw-nag'). It means to be soft, delicate, pampered, and dainty. It also means to be happy about, and to take exquisite delight in. `Anag also means to be of dainty habit; to make merry over, or to make sport of. Delight means to take or give great pleasure, or joy, to rejoice, exult, please, and to make gladden.

God wants us to delight in Him. God is waiting to give His people the desires of their hearts. The desires of His peoples' hearts are his desires that He placed there. When I delight in the Lord I seek to please Him. I begin to rejoice, spin around, leap, laugh, as I am made glad. When we delight ourselves before the LORD, we are playing before Him. We are rejoicing, and shouting! We are celebrating, praising, and worshiping Him!

God wants us to dance and play before Him. We are God's children. He sits on His throne, looking upon His people, as we play before Him. As we worship Him in the beauty of holiness, as we sing, as we dance, praise, and worship Him, let God be pleased as we laugh, jest, and play before Him!

Let's go out, and play in His presence. Let's go and play, as we praise, and worship God. Let's go and play, as we practice the presence of God, and worship Him in spirit and in truth! Let's delight in our Mighty God! We are in His hands, under His feathers, **in His playpen!** No harm can come to us.

LET US PLAY!

*The earth revolving around the sun is like a worshipper revolving around the Son. The closer you are to the Son the warmer you are. The farther you get from the Son, the colder you get.*

*Worship produces sweet honey.*

*Worship is warship.*

# CHAPTER TWELVE

# LAUGHTER IN THE SPIRIT

"When the LORD turned again the captivity of Zion, we were like them that dream. Then was **our mouth filled with laughter**, and our tongue with singing: then said they among the heathen, The LORD hath done great things for them. The LORD hath done great things for us; whereof, we are glad. Turn again our captivity, O LORD, as the streams in the south. They that sow in tears shall reap in joy. He that goeth forth and weepeth, bearing precious seed, shall doubtless come again with rejoicing, bringing his sheaves with him." Psalm 126.

"He that sitteth in the heavens shall laugh: the Lord shall have them in derision." Psalm 2:4. "The Lord shall laugh at him: for he seeth that his day is coming." Psalm 37:13. "But thou, O LORD, shalt laugh at them; thou shalt have all the heathen in derision." Psalm 59:8.

**God's People are Laughing because they are FREE!**

All over the land, laughter is invading the body of Christ. We are dancing, singing, praying, bowing, kneeling, clapping, jumping, leaping, shouting, spinning, praising, worshiping, and **now we're laughing!** We're laughing in the spirit. Our spirit man is laughing!

The Spirit of God is invading us! To be invaded means to enter by force in order to conquer; intrude, or overrun. Laughter is expressing certain emotions, especially mirth, delight, or derision, by a series of spontaneous, usually unarticulated sounds often accompanied by corresponding facial, and sometimes bodily movements. Laughter also means to feel a triumphant or exultant sense of well-being. We laugh at something amusing, absurd, or something contemptible; or a joke. The Spirit of God is laughing through His people today! The laughter is attributed to several responses.

In Psalm 126, the Jews were coming out of captivity in Babylon, and returning home to Jerusalem. The Jews could not believe that they had been set free! Verse 1 portrayed them as walking like they were in a dream! They could not believe it! Finally, they were set free! After desiring so long to be loosed from bondage, after desiring so long to be free from captivity, after desiring so long to return back to Jerusalem, it's like a dream, finally they were free!

As they walked, their mouths were filled with laughter, their tongues were filled with singing, and their hearts were glorifying God! They were laughing! Laughing! Laughing! Laughing! They were laughing because they were FREE!

This is one reason why today laughter is infesting the body of Christ, because we have been loosed, we are FREE! We are not in bondage, but we are FREE! We are not bound by the power of the devil, but we are FREE! The devil has piped unto us, and we have not danced; but we are dancing, and laughing because we are FREE! We are dancing unto the Lord, and not unto the devil! Matt. 11:17 says, "And saying, We have piped unto you, and ye have not danced; we have mourned unto you, and ye have not lamented." We are FREE!

God has given us our breakthroughs! God has edified His people! God has encouraged, and built His people up, so that they can stand. We are so overwhelmed with God's daily mercy, His grace, His love, His power, His provision, His compassion, and His divine pity, that we are laughing; laughing in the Spirit!

### God Laughing Through His People

"He that sitteth in the heavens shall laugh: the Lord shall have them in derision." Psalm 2:4. "The Lord shall laugh at him: for he seeth that his day is coming." Psalm 37:13. "But thou, O LORD, shalt laugh at them; thou shalt have all the heathen in derision." Psalm 59:8.

In each of these verses, the word laugh is the Hebrew word "sachaq," pronounced (saw-khak'). Its Hebrew meaning is to laugh, play, or to mock. Sachaq also means to laugh usually in contempt, or derision; to sport, jest, or play. Ironically, to play also includes instrumental music, singing, and dancing. SELAH!

As God dwell in the heavens, and dwell in the hearts of His people, He prays through them, He preaches through them, and He sings. God plays, worships and speaks through His people, well He also LAUGHS!

### HA, HA, HAAAAAAAAAAAHHHH!!!!!!!!!

But why is God laughing? Psalm 2 says that God is sitting back laughing because the kings, and the rulers of the earth are taking counsel together against the LORD, and against God's anointed!

Our enemies are making plans against God, and against God's anointed! God is laughing because He sees their calamity coming. The Lord shall laugh at him: for he seeth that his day is coming. Psalm 37:13.

In Isaiah 46:10, God declares the end from the beginning! He sees the soon destruction of our enemies.

He sees our enemies planning against us, but He's laughing! He sees our enemies plotting, sneaking, whispering, and scheming against His anointed, but God is laughing! They are surmising their plan of action against us in their secret closets! They come up with impractical, unrealistic, devious, satanic, demonic, secret plans and plots against us, yet GOD IS LAUGHING!

Why are the people of God laughing? We are laughing because God is laughing! God is laughing because He sees the destruction, and end of our enemies! We are laughing because God is laughing through us! We are not laughing, but it is God laughing through us! It is not by our power that we are laughing, but it is by God's power, through His Spirit!

The laughter in the earth, is an illustration of what is happening in the heavenlies! Our enemies are defeated, and we are laughing! Our enemies are under our feet, and we are laughing! Our enemies are our footstool, and we are laughing! We are authorized to command evil, demonic, and contrary spirits to get back, to loose our families, our finances, our jobs, our churches, and our health, and we are laughing! We know that we will win in every affliction, and we are laughing! "Many are the afflictions of the righteous: but the LORD delivereth him out of them all." Psalm 34:19.

We are laughing because Matthew 18:18 says "Whatsoever ye shall bind on earth shall be bound in heaven: and whatsoever ye shall loose on earth shall be loosed in heaven." We are laughing because the victory is ours! We do not have to wait to see the outcome, and then shout, but we can shout now. We can laugh now! The victory is ours! The victory is yours! Laugh and keep on laughing!

### TOUCH NOT GOD'S ANOINTED!

When our enemies plot, and scheme against us, they are plotting against the Lord. This proof is found in Acts 9, with Saul. "And Saul, yet breathing out threatenings and slaughter against the disciples of the Lord, went unto the high priest. And desired of him letters to Damascus to the synagogues, that if he found any of this way, whether they were men or women, he might bring them bound unto Jerusalem. And as he journeyed, he came near Damascus: and suddenly there shined round about him a light from heaven: And he fell to the earth, and heard a voice saying unto him, Saul, Saul, why persecutest thou me?"

Although Saul, was on his way to threaten, and to slaughter the disciples of the Lord, the question God asked him was not, Saul, Saul, why persecutest thou my disciples, **BUT** why persecutest **thou me? No doubt, this means that when plots, and schemes come against you from your enemies, that they are literally plotting, attacking, and scheming against God!** That is why God is laughing through us! They plot against me, yet they are plotting against God.

I laugh because not only is God sitting in the heavens laughing because He sees our enemies' end coming, **but I see it too!** Therefore, I am laughing too! I begin to rejoice! Vengeance belongeth unto the Lord. He will repay! "For it is written, Vengeance is mine; **I will repay**, saith the Lord." Romans 12: 19.    The Lord God Almighty will repay. The omnipotent, potent, high God shall repay!

Observe what Matthew 5: 11-16 says, "Blessed are ye, when men shall revile you, and persecute you, and shall say all manner of evil against you falsely, for my sake. **Rejoice, and be** exceeding glad: for great is your reward in heaven: for so persecuted they the prophets which were before you. Ye are the salt of the earth: but if the salt have lost his savor, wherewith shall it be salted? It is thenceforth good for nothing, but to be cast out, and to be trodden under foot of men. Ye are the light of the world. A city that is set on a hill cannot be hid.    Neither do men light a candle, and put it under a bushel, but on a candlestick; and it giveth light unto all that are in the house.    Let your light so shine before men, that they may see your good works, and glorify your Father which is in heaven."

This passage tells us to rejoice and be exceeding glad when our enemies revile us, persecute us, and say all manner of evil against us falsely, for His sake. **Be glad, laugh, laugh, laugh, and keep on laughing! That's where your victory lies!**

**If you decide to attack your enemies, you have lost!** You lose your salt savor, and then your light from within you grows dim, until it goes out. When you decide to take matters in your own hand and try to destroy your enemies yourself, you lose your savor, and your light grows dim.    Do not take matters in your own hand! Do not do this!    This is a warning!    This is highly dangerous!    Be still and know that God is God!

Let God take them out, if He chooses! Matthew 5:44 says, "But I say unto you, Love your enemies, **bless them that curse** you, do good to **them that** hate you, and pray for **them** which despitefully use you, and persecute you."

Romans 12: 20 says, "Therefore if thine enemy hunger, feed him; if he thirst, give him drink: for in so doing thou shalt **heap coals** of fire on his head." Your enemies cannot take your kindness, and your blessings toward them!    Keep on laughing!

I Chronicles 16:22 says, "[Saying], **Touch not** mine **anointed**, and do **my** prophets no harm."

God warns our enemies about their faulty plans against us.  Their plans against us, are plans against God.  Touch not, handle not, plot not, scheme not, whisper not, conspire not, connive not, harm not... saith the LORD!

In I Chronicles 13: 8-10, God had already warned the people about touching the ark, less they die.  Observe what happens to one if they touch the ark....

"And David and all Israel played before God with all [their] might, and with singing, and with harps, and with psalteries, and with timbrels, and with cymbals, and with trumpets.  And when they came unto the threshingfloor of Chidon, **Uzza put forth his hand to hold the ark**; for the oxen stumbled.  **And the anger of the LORD was kindled against Uzza, and he smote him, because he put his hand to the ark: and there he died before God.**"

Again God is saying, Touch not the anointed!  Touch not the anointed things of God!  There are deadly consequences in touching the anointed things of God!  There can be deadly consequences!

Psalm 37 says that evildoers will be cut off; for yet a little while, and the wicked shall not be: yea, thou shalt diligently consider his place, and it shall not be.  This passage also states that the seed of the wicked shall be cut off(vs. 28).  Because of the actions of our enemies, some of our enemies' seed is cut off, because of their plots against the anointed of God!  WATCH OUT!  WATCH IT!  LOOK OUT!  Touch not the anointed of God!

THIS IS A WARNING!  To our enemies:  your plots are deadly!  Your words enter your own heart!  They return unto you.  Your words directed at us, comes back around like a boomerang, and pierces your heart with your own words!  A sword into the heart can be dangerous, wounding, hurtful, painful, and deadly!

In the Amplified Bible, Isaiah 41:10-13 says, "Fear not; there is nothing to fear for I am with you; do not look around you in terror and be dismayed, for I am your God.  I will strengthen and harden you to difficulties; yes, I will help you; yes, I will hold you up and retain you with my victorious right hand of rightness and justice.  Behold, all they who are enrages and inflamed against you shall be put to shame and confounded; they who strive against you shall be as nothing and shall perish.  You shall seek those who contend with you, and shall not find them; they who war against you shall be as nothing, as nothing at all.  For I, the Lord you God, hold your right hand; I, Who say to you, Fear not, I will help you!"

God is saying that He will make you harden to difficulties, that is, He will cause difficulties to bounce right off of you. Do not be afraid. You will look around one day, and your enemies will be gone! They will be transferred, dismissed, and dismayed! Their time is almost up, and over! Fear not!

"Fret not thyself because of evildoers, neither be thou envious against the workers of iniquity. *The Lord shall laugh at him: for he seeth that his day is coming.*" Psalm 37.

The LORD is laughing.....His people are laughing....It's the sound of the voice of God in the earth....It's the sound of victory....It's the sound of a sure end to the plots of our enemies....It's a sound of God's victory on our behalf....It's the sound of gladness, joy, and happiness, knowing that our enemies are defeated!!! For the battle is not ours, but the LORD'S!!!

**WE ARE FREE.....AND WE ARE LAUGHING!!!!**

Ha, Ha, Ha, Ha, Ha, Ha, Ha, He, He, He, Ha, HAAAAAAAAAAAAAAAH!!!!!!!

"Behold, I will do **a new thing**; now it shall spring forth; shall ye not know it? I will even make **a** way in the wilderness, [and] rivers in the desert." Isaiah 43:19.

# Ceaseless Worship!

*Worship is like rain, it descends from heaven, then
like dew it transcends, –evaporates– back
into the heart of the Father.*

*Worship is my living sacrifice unto the Lord.*

*Worship is like taking a flight on a cloudy day,
the higher you rise and ascend above the
clouds, the more you see the Son(sun).*

# CHAPTER THIRTEEN

# BASKING IN THE SON (SUN)

"Thou wilt shew me the path of life: in thy **presence** is fulness of joy; at thy right hand there are pleasures for evermore." Psalm 16:11.

Basking is exposing yourself to pleasant warmth. It is taking great pleasure or satisfaction in resting, or relaxation. Basking is to allow yourself to indulge, wallow, or to luxuriate in something. Basking in the sun, is lying in the sun enjoying its warmth. It is indulging yourself!

As you lie on the beach enjoying the sun, I admonish you to lie before God, enjoying His Son. As you bask in the sun, bask in the Son! Bow, then kneel, then just lie prostrate before the Lord enjoying His presence. Enjoy the heat of His presence! Enjoy the comfort of the presence of God! Strip before Him! Be transparent, honest, and open before Him. Be revealing to Him! Lie before Him! Enjoy and meditate upon who He is! Enthrone Him upon your heart. Gaze upon Him! Behold Him in all His beauty. Worship Him in the beauty of holiness. Adore His splendid brilliance!

Behold God in all of His glory! Let Him rain upon you. Let His light shine upon you! Let Him tan your image with His Son! Let His presence change you on the inside, and the outside. Let Him conform, and transform you into the image of His dear Son.

**Bake in His presence! Tan in His presence! Worship in His presence! Lie prostrate before Him! Bask in the Son! Bask in God's presence! Get a Son tan!**

Basking in God's presence is exposing yourself to His presence, His will, His purpose, His judgments, His destiny, His mind, His power, His path, His way, His thoughts, His radiance, and His glory. God's glory is a summation of all of who He is.

I want to expose myself to Him. I want to indulge myself in His presence. I want to bake in His presence. I want to be changed, and transformed in His presence.

I want to be with Him, and in Him. Christ in me the hope of glory. My life is hid in Him. My heart wants to wallow in Him. I want to take extravagant pleasure in my Lord's presence. I want God to love me; to speak to me; to reveal Himself to me; to comfort me; to console me; to pamper me; to hold me; and to embrace me. As He surrounds me with His presence, He holds me, and embraces me.

"As the hart **panteth** after the water brooks, so **panteth** my soul after thee, O God." Psalm 42:1. My heart longeth for the presence of God. Before God's presence, stands all of me, all of my desires, my longings, all of my issues of my life. In God's presence, my shortcomings, misfortunes, mistakes, and fears, are ever before Him. "Lord, all my desire is before thee; and my groaning is not hid from thee. My heart **panteth**, my strength faileth me: as for the light of mine eyes, it also is gone from me." Psalm 38:9, 10. As I am in God's presence, my heart palpitates because my God is an all consuming fire! I'm breathless! I lie in awe of Him.

My longing is to hear His voice speak to me. I long to hear His voice. I long to see His visions. My heart's desire is that He will speak. Holy, Holy, Holy is the LORD OF HOSTS! Speak Lord, thy servant heareth.

As you bask in His presence, God will begin to speak your purpose unto you. He opens up your understanding, and pours revelations, visions, His word, and dreams into you. Your destiny is spoken over you by the very voice of God. God's voice is still, soft and quiet, yet audible. God's voice is mighty! God's voice is powerful! Read Psalm 29.

In the presence of the Lord there is fulness of joy. There is much joy, much love, much richness, much wealth, much abundance, and much power.

'Fulness' is the Hebrew word "soba`," pronounced (so'-bah). Soba means to have an abundance, or satiety. To have an abundance is to have plenty, and to be bounteous in all things. When you abound in all things, you are made rich.

An abundance is large in number, or yield. To abound in all things is to be great in number, or amount; to be fully supplied, filled; or teem. To be teem is to be full of things, to the extent of being swarmed by an influx of it. To be teem is to be or become pregnant; to bear or produce young. Teeming is coming or going in large numbers. It's pouring much in; it's flooding you with an influx of blessings. It's a massive outpouring of the blessings of God by the Spirit of God upon your life.

In God's presence, you conceive seed. As you become one with God, You become impregnated with His Word. Visions are produced in the presence of the Lord. Destiny is opened unto you in His presence. His Word is birthed within you. Out of your belly will flow rivers of living water, living word, living power, and living anointing.

"Furthermore then we beseech you, brethren, and exhort you by the Lord Jesus, that as ye have received of us how ye ought to walk and to please God, so ye would **abound more and more.**" I Th. 4:1. In this verse, to abound is to exceed a fixed number. It is to go over, to be in abundance, to be great, to have an overflow, to exceed, or excel. To abound is when something falls to the lot of one in a large measure. Abounding is to be in affluence; to furnish one richly, so that he has an abundance.

To abound is to be made excellent. When you are made to be excellent, you are of the highest or finest quality. You are made to be exceptionally good. You become superior in the human sense. God makes you to be great, in His time! **Will you bask in His presence?** You become first-class, and first rate! You become a champion! You're topflight. You will be well above your average peers around you. Bask in His presence! Love Him. You will become high-grade! You will be first. Bask in His presence. Bond with God. You will be fully furnished with all things. You will have an overflow, because you have basked, dwelt, and abided in the presence of the Lord. People will compliment you. Their compliments are really God's compliments.

You will abound more and more in the presence of the Lord. You will increase more and more. I Thessalonians 4: 10. **There are no substitutes for God's presence!** God will cause you to abound to a larger and greater degree. To abound more and more means that you will have much, by far. You will excel, and increase. Bask in His presence.

Abounding is best illustrated as a flower going from a bud to full bloom. When you abound, you blossom wherever you are. You bloom! You come forth shining bright, glowing, growing, flourishing, expanding, and increasing more and more.

"Those that be planted in the house of the LORD shall flourish in the courts of our God." Psalm 92:13. Your body is the temple of God. Your body is the house of God. Dwell in the Most Holy Place. FLOURISH IN THE COURTS OF OUR GOD. FLOURISH IN THE MOST HOLY PLACE OF GOD IN YOUR TEMPLE, IN THE COURTS OF OUR GOD.

In the presence of the Lord you increase, you grow, you shine, you glow, you are made rich, you prosper, you expand, you exceed, you excel, you achieve, you are impregnated, you are filled, you blossom, you bloom, you flourish, you spring forth, and you are empowered. You will increase more and more!

You will outshine, outdo, out smart, out-think, and outgrow those around you. God's presence is supernatural, miraculous, beyond any conceivable expression known to man. BASK IN HIS PRESENCE! BASK IN HIS GLORY! If God is supernatural, then supernatural things will occur in His presence, as you bask in the Son. If God is powerful, and miraculous, then powerful and miraculous things will transpire in His presence. I want to bask in His presence.

As we dwell in God's presence, we behold His glory. "But we all, with open face beholding as in a glass the glory of the Lord, are changed into the same image from glory to glory, even as by the Spirit of the Lord." I Cor. 3:18.

As we bask in God's presence, we are changed! No man can go into the presence of the Lord and remain the same. Everything must change. Nothing stays the same. Bask in His presence. Bask in His glory. Bask in His majesty. Bask in His peace. Bask in His love. Bask in His anointing. Bask in His power. Bask in His joy. Bask in His abundance. Bask in His warmth. Bask in His fire! For our God is a consuming fire! Bask. Swim. Indulge. Wallow. Rest. Live. Dwell. Abide. Walk. Work. Bask. Bask. Bask. Bask in His presence. Bask in His cloud.

**The Cycle of the Worshipper Getting to Know God**

*Holiness is the key to worship.*

*Worship will not return unto you void. God is a rewarder of them that diligently seek Him.*

*Worship is ministering unto the Lord.*

# CHAPTER FOURTEEN

# MY NAME IS JEALOUS!

### Jehovah Kanna

"So the angel that communed with me said unto me, Cry thou, saying, Thus saith the LORD of hosts; I am **jealous** for Jerusalem and for Zion with a great jealousy." Zec 1:14

"For thou shalt worship no other god: for the LORD, whose name *is* **Jealous,** *is* a **jealous** God." Ex. 34:14.

"Thou shalt not bow down thyself to them, nor serve them: for I the LORD thy God *is* a **jealous** God, visiting the iniquity of the fathers upon the children unto the third and fourth *generation* of them that hate me." Ex. 20:5.

Our God is an awesome God! Our God is more than awesome! Our God is far more than awesome! Our God is infinitely awesome; yet, He is a jealous God! God says to His nation of people...

"I am jealous towards you with a godly jealousy. You shall not bow down thyself to other idols, nor serve them: for I the LORD thy God am a jealous God. Thou shalt worship no other god: for I, the LORD, whose name is JEALOUS, is a jealous God. My glory will I not give to another. Thou shalt have no other gods beside me. Thou shall not make unto you any graven images! I the Lord declare to generations that I want you. I am your God! I am the first. I am the last. I am the beginning. I am the end.

I want to be first. I am preeminent, but not in your life. Knoweth thou not that I am the first. That is, I want to be first in your time schedule, first in your heart, first in your giving of your finances, first in your thoughts, first to come to your mind as you awaken each day, the first for you to consult, first in counseling and advising you, first in receiving thanks from you, first to be worshipped, first in the sharing of love in your heart, first in your life before your spouse, before your friends, before your confidants; yes, I the LORD GOD, JEHOVAH KANNA, am the first and not the second. My glory will I not share with any other! Return to your first love.

My heart bleeds when you put others first, when you place them before me. My heart pours tears when you abandon me for someone else. My heart palpitates when you enthrone others in my place. NO! That's my place! NO! That's my spot! NO! That's my seat! NO! That's my throne! NO! That's my time! I come to turn over anything, or anybody that occupies MY PLACE!

Thou shalt have no other anything before me! I come to drive out things that have the wrong place in your life, or in your temple! "And when he had made a scourge of small cords, he drove them all out of the temple, and the sheep, and the oxen; and poured out the changers' money, and overthrew the tables...." John 2:15.

Do you realize that when you place others' opinions before me, others' love before me that you have made graven images unto yourself? Do you realize when you spend more time with others than you spend with me that they can become an idol? Graven images? Idolatry? Idol worship? False worship? False gods? Graven people? Graven possessions? A false balance? It's an abomination unto me. It is equated into a false balance! I supply your needs, desires, wants, etc.

"Thou shalt have no other gods before me. Thou shalt not make unto thee any graven image, or any likeness *of any thing* that is in heaven above, or that is in the earth beneath, or that is in the water under the earth. Thou shalt not bow down thyself to them, nor serve them: for I the LORD thy God *am* a jealous God, visiting the iniquity of the fathers upon the children unto the third and fourth *generation* of them that hate me. And shewing mercy unto thousands of them that love me, and keep my commandments." Exodus 20:3-6.

Thou shalt have NO other person before me! Thou shalt have no other child, spouse, friend, job, hobby, ministry, business, desire, or any plan before me! My name is JEALOUS!

It was I that brought you out of the land of bondage. It was I that brought you out of the shackles of sin. I destroyed the yokes in your life that possessed, and had a grip on you. I untied, and loosed you. I made a way of escape from temptations for you. I chase away your enemies. I was crucified for you. I died for you. I deserve first place in your life.

It was I that fed you. It was I that was there with you in the valley. It was I that was with you through your sickness. It's me! I am your God. I am your provision. I am your protection, and shield. I defend you. I guard you. I guide you. I comfort you. I hold you. I hug you. I kiss you. I surround you. I embrace you. I minister unto you. I order your steps. I create, and open doors and windows for you. I love you more than anyone can ever dream, or think of. It is I that doeth all these things, plus a zillion more. I even move you! "For in him(me) **you live, and move**, and **have your being**." Acts 17:26.

I give you desires of your heart, visions, dreams, revelations, wisdom, knowledge and understanding.

You sit in heavenly places. You have not chosen me, but I have chosen you. You are mine. You are complete in me. You are a new creation. Your life is hid in me. You are united with me. I am married to you. I am your husband, your sweetheart, and a gentleman.

I am the only one who knows the number of hairs upon your head. I am the only one to know all of thy downsittings and thy uprisings. I only understandest thy thought from afar off. I encompasseth your paths, and your lying down. I, only, am acquainted with all of your ways. I covered you in your mother's womb. My thoughts of you are more than the sands of the sea. I think of you all the day long. It is my eye that beholds, and watches over you. I created you. I breathed into your nostrils the breath of life.

The oxygen is mine. The air is mine. The breath is mine. The blood is mine! I am the possessor of all things. "For the earth is the Lord's and the fullness thereof, the world, and they that dwell therein." Psalm 24:1. "And he is before all things, and by him all things **consist**." Colossians 1:17.

Consist means that I place things together, and cause them to stick, and stay together. It is I that set one with another. I introduce you to myself. It is I that unite separate parts together, so that they become one, and stay one. It is I that cause things to stick together, and to work and function the way that I have ordained and commanded it to be.

I perform the miracles. I heal. I set you free. I grant victories, and deliverances. I exalt, and abase. I promote. I send the rain. I send the increase. I send the prosperity. I send the abundance. I cause you to reap. I the Lord doeth all these things towards you.

I am jealous over you. I have chosen you. I have made you beautiful in your time. I have made you kings, priests, queens, princes, princesses, and heirs to my throne. Your price is far above rubies. I paid that price for you. I bought you. You are my treasure. You are my precious jewels. You are my precious stones. You are heirs, and joint-heirs with me and my Son. You are royal, and regal. You are majestic. You are rich, and wealthy. You are like pure gold. You are in my royal family, and a member of my royal priesthood. You are from a royal lineage, because you are mine, and I am rich, and royal! Everything belongs to me, for it was I who created the world, and everything in it.

You are mine, and I am your beloved! I love you with an everlasting, non-separating, non-abandoning, unconditional love. I love you. You belong to me. You are mine. You are the apple of my eye. You are my heartbeat. I want you. You are mine! I am jealous over you! My name is *JEHOVAH KANNA*, THE GOD WHO IS JEALOUS OVER YOU! LOVE ME!"

*Worship births life.*

*Worship is adoration*

# CHAPTER FIFTEEN

# GOD, A LIVING SANCTUARY

"Therefore say, Thus saith the Lord GOD; Although I have cast them far off among the heathen, and although I have scattered them among the countries, **yet will I be to them as a little sanctuary in the countries where they shall come.**" Ezekiel 11:16.

"And I saw **no temple** therein: **for the Lord God Almighty and the Lamb are the temple of it.**" Revelation 21:22.

"They shall enter into my sanctuary, and they shall come near to my table, **to minister unto me**, and they shall keep my charge." Ezekiel 44:16.

"To see thy power and thy glory, so as I have seen thee in the sanctuary." Psalm 63:2.

In Ezekiel 11:16, God promised that He would be a little sanctuary unto His people. This sanctuary is described as the Most Holy Place of God. It is that hallowed place! This sanctuary is that sacred, sanctified place in God. It is the sanctuary of Jehovah! It is Jehovah, Himself, a living sanctuary!

God is a sanctuary. Many of us seek to routinely go to church, the temple, each week; but God wants to be that sanctuary that you come to and worship. He wants us to come unto Him to worship, and to minister unto Him.

**We prefer going to the local assembly, more than going directly to God as a sanctuary.** We rely too much on going to church for help, and to hear a word from God; when we need to realize that God prefers us to seek Him, and come to Him as if He is the living sanctuary itself. Come to Him in times of trouble. Come to Him as a sanctuary to hear a word from God. He wants us to dwell in Him, to live and reside in Him; that is, in His sanctuary.

**Cherish coming to God as a sanctuary, more than going to the local church. It is fine to attend church; however, make your priority to go to God as the sanctuary, more than going to your local assembly.**

His sanctuary is a secret, sweet, sacred, holy, hallowed place. "He that dwelleth in the secret place of the most High shall abide under the shadow of the Almighty. Because thou hast made the LORD, which is my refuge, even the most High, thy habitation." Psalm 91:1, 9. "The name of the LORD is a strong tower: the righteous runneth into it, and is safe." Proverbs 18:10. "Lord, thou hast been our dwelling place in all generations." Psalm 90:1. "And he shall be for a sanctuary...." Isaiah 8:14.

You see, we need to catch a glimpse of God being a place of refuge, shelter, and covering for us. He desires you to come unto Him daily, as if you are going to your local church. Come unto Him. He is the sanctuary. And as you continually enter God's presence, you will begin to minister unto the Lord! "They shall enter into my sanctuary, and they shall come near to my table, to minister unto me, and they shall keep my charge." Ezekiel 44:16.

In Revelation 21:22, there you find God declaring that in the end, in that heavenly place, that there will no longer be a need for temples to be erected, for the Lord God Almighty and the Lamb are the temple of it. **This means that God Almighty, and the Lamb is the temple itself. This means that God Almighty, and the Lamb is the living sanctuary itself for the kingdom of God to come and worship in.**

People will no longer have a need to go to a building to worship, for the Lamb and God Almighty is the sanctuary. They will come unto the Lord God Almighty and the Lamb to worship.

The presence of God makes the sanctuary, and it is not the sanctuary that secures the presence. His presence is a sanctuary.

God is the best, ultimate, highest sanctuary for you to go to and attend regularly. You must have more than bricks, mortar, stainglassed windows, padded pews, organs and instruments, microphones, and pulpits; but you must have God as your Sanctuary, all of Him. He is a living sanctuary. He is our house of worship. He gives us a house, or dwelling place to worship. He is the house of worship, and guess what, He comes too! "For where two or three are gathered together in my name, there am I in the midst of them." Matthew 18:20. In this case, the two or three includes the Father, Son, Holy Ghost, and of course, YOU!

Therefore, if God's presence is the sanctuary, and He's everywhere, then when I become aware of His presence, I appear in the sanctuary of the Most High. Wherever and whenever God comes upon us and makes Himself known to us, there He makes a sanctuary. When this happens, watch out; you are on holy ground!

"And the Word was made flesh, and **dwelt[tabernacled] among us,** (and we beheld his glory, the glory as of the only begotten of the Father,) full of grace and truth." John 1:14.

**Worship God in His sanctuary.**

*Worship loosens you from Satan's*
*grip. Worship destroys yokes!*

*Worship declares the glory of God.*

# CHAPTER SIXTEEN

# REHOBOTH…A PLACE OF REST

" **A** nd he removed from thence, and digged another well; and
for that they strove not: and he called the name of it
**Rehoboth**; and he said, For now **the LORD hath made room for us,
and we shall be fruitful in the land.**" Genesis 26:22.

Are you tired? Do you need rest? Well, the word "Rehoboth"
is defined as an open, broad, spaced room of rest. God is my open
place of rest. This room has been made especially for me. Not only
does God promise to make room for us, but He also promised that
we shall be fruitful in the land. For now **the LORD hath made room
for us, and we shall be fruitful in the land.**" Genesis 26:22.

"Come unto me, all that labor and are heavy laden, **and I will
give you rest.** Take my yoke upon you, and learn of me; for I am
meek and lowly in heart: and ye shall find rest unto your souls.
For my yoke is easy, and my burden is light." Matthew 11:28-30.

We will enter God's rest when we begin to fully trust in the
Lord knowing that He is our shield and protection. When God is

my shield, I trust in Him completely, and I believe that God is in full control of the situation that I may fear, then I enter into God's rest. When I fear, and am dismayed, then I have not entered God's rest. When I am troubled, and I begin to worry about what is going to happen, or what has happened, then I cannot enter God's rest. Before I enter rest, I must come unto Jesus. Jesus says, "Come unto me." Come, and rest!

### Rest Upon Me, O Lord, Rest Upon Me

**Foxes have holes, birds of the air have nest, but the Son of Man has not where to lay His head. Luke 9:58.** God assures us rest, if we come unto Him. On the other hand, the Son of Man is looking for somewhere or someplace for Him to lay His head.

Our response should be to Jesus, rest upon me O Lord, rest upon me. I want God's Spirit to rest upon me. God is looking for a dwelling place to make His abode. God is looking for some place to lay His head. A head can be viewed as a place of authority. If you are the head of anything, you definitely have a place of authority. God is looking for someone to lay His authority upon, a person totally controlled by Him, and submitted to Him.

I want the Spirit of God to hover over me, to overwhelm, and to overshadow me. "And the Spirit of God moved upon the face of the waters." Genesis 1:2. To move upon the waters is to hover over them, to relax on them, and to stay there. Father, hover over me. Relax yourself on me. Move upon the altars of my heart and mind.

"I saw the Spirit descending from heaven like a dove, and it **abode upon him.** And I knew him not: but he that sent me to baptize with water, the same said unto me, upon whom thou shalt see the Spirit **descending, and remaining on him,** the same is he which baptizeth with the Holy Ghost." John 1:32, 33.

To *abode* means that the Spirit of God abided, dwelt, remained, and tarried upon Jesus. Allow the Spirit of God to abode upon you, to stay and remain upon you in order to empower you for service. This empowers you for signs, miracles and wonders. Unbelievable things will begin to happen to you.

Not only do I seek His Spirit, but also I seek His power, His anointing, His blessings, His prosperity, His love, His grace, His mercy, His goodness, and His blood **to rest upon me.**

The Lord inhabiteth the praises of His people. So we need to praise Him so He can come and inhabit our praises, and then rest upon us.

**My prayer is that you will not respond by saying that there is no room in the inn.** "And she brought forth her firstborn son, and wrapped him in swaddling clothes, and laid him in a manger; because there was no room for them in the inn." Luke 2:7.

"Come unto me, all that labor and are heavy laden, **and I will give you rest.** Take my yoke upon you, and learn of me; for I am meek and lowly in heart: **and ye shall find rest unto your souls.** For my yoke is easy, and my burden is light." Matthew 11:28-30.

God gives us an invitation to come unto Him and rest; however, He wants to also be able to rest His head upon you! **Foxes have holes, birds of the air have nest,** but the Son of Man has not where to lay His head. **Luke 9:58.**

# COME...

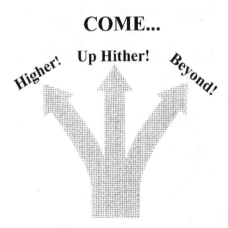

**New Directions & Dimensions the Worshipper is Beckon to Walk**

Come Up Hither; Come Higher; Come Beyond

91

*Worship brings peace.*

*Worship is my treasure in heaven.*

## CHAPTER SEVENTEEN

# THE SECRET PLACE
# THE SACRED PLACE

He that dwelleth in the **secret place** of the most High shall   abide under the shadow of the Almighty." Psalm 91:1.

"Keep me as the apple of the eye, hide me **under the shadow of thy wings**...." Psalm 17:8.

"For in the time of trouble **he shall hide me in his pavilion: in the secret of his tabernacle shall he hide me**; he shall set me up upon a rock.   And now shall mine head be lifted up above mine enemies round about me...." Psalm 27: 5, 6a.

The secret place?  The sacred place?  What is it?  Where is it? How do I find this place in God?

### The Secret Place in the Tabernacle

In Exodus 25-27, and 35-38, there lies an explanation of what the tabernacle should look like, along with its furniture.  The tabernacle represented the presence of God.  It stood for God's dwelling place on earth. It stood for a pattern, copy and shadow of heavenly things in heaven.

When the tabernacle was reviewed, it had three compartments. These compartments were namely, the outer court, the inner court, and the innermost court. Other names given to these compartments are the outer court, the Holy Place, and the Most Holy Place, also known as the Holy of Holies. Other names are respectively: the first, and second tabernacle.

In the outer court, it was a place where animals were to be slain, and offered as sacrifices unto the LORD. In the outer court, there was also the laver. The laver was a place of washing, and cleansing. The priest would wash his hands and feet before offering any sacrifices. This area was the largest area of the tabernacle.

In the inner court, the priest would enter the Holy Place and perform several duties. He would trim the wicks on the lampstand, and place oil in them. He would also ensure that incense was placed in the altar of incense, and would replace the shewbread on the Sabbath day, afterwards, eating the old bread that was there.

**The main point to the secret place lies in the Holy of Holies.** *The Holy of Holies was* measured as a perfect cube. It was 15 feet by 15 feet by 15 feet. It had only one piece of furniture in the Holy of Holies, and that was the Ark of the Covenant. The Ark of the Covenant represented the presence, nature, and the character of God.

The point is that the Holy of Holies was a secret place! No one was allowed to enter this place, except the High Priest, and that entrance was done only on the Day of Atonement. This happened only once a year. The Innermost place (Holy of Holies) was the place farthest within the tabernacle. It was a place of secrecy from all twelve tribes, including the priest, and the levites. Because no one except the high priest could enter this place, it was known as a secret, sacred, sanctified, sweet, divine, consecrated, hallowed, devoted, and Most holy place. It was known as a place where God dwelt, and resided. It was known as the place where the Shekinah glory of God, which represented the Holy Spirit of God, manifested Himself. The Spirit was the glory of the Shekinah presence of God.

The secret place was a place hidden, and concealed from the congregation of the people. It was a secret place. It was a sacred place. It was a holy place. They could not see the  inside of this place. It was hidden. It was a secret. They could not see what went on even on the Day of Atonement on the inside. The Day of Atonement is known as a day of '*at-one-ment*' with God. They could only visualize, and imagine what was going on. The priest had taught the people the process of atonement in their daily teachings.

The people could not hear the bells on the end of the high priest's garment on this day because the high priest went in into the Holy of Holies with only a linen garment on. On the other hand, the people however, did hear the bells continuously as the priest, and high priest ministered in the holy place daily.

The people also could not see the lighted compartment within the Holy of Holies, shining upon the Ark of the Covenant, upon the mercy seat. They could not see God's presence wrapped around the ark. The presence of God brought light to the dark room of the Holy of Holies. God's presence brought light to the secret place.

The people could only sense the satisfaction of God, and how He was pleased as the high priest sprinkled blood upon the mercy seat. They could only feel a sense of relief as the blood was sprinkled upon the mercy seat. They felt a sense of forgiveness and cleanliness. If the high priest survived the sprinkling, then there was a release of the scapegoat. Their sins had been covered, or atoned for another year. God accepted the blood sacrifice.

In this *secret room*, it was very dark. It was only lighted when the Shekinah glory of God would overshadow the room with great light, and great power. The Shekinah glory represented the Holy Spirit. It was known as the visible presence, or radiance of God. The glory is sometimes called a cloud. It is known as the dwelling of God. The glory of God illuminated light within the room. **But this room was a secret, sacred, holy place.** It was the meeting place of God, or the throne of God. This was a place of communion, Holy Communion. "And there I will meet with thee, and I will commune with thee from above the mercy seat, from between the two cherubims which are upon the ark of the testimony, of all things which I will give thee in commandment unto the children of Israel." Exodus 25:22.

**When the glory cloud fell upon the tabernacle, it represents the Holy Spirit of God falling upon us today. The Spirit falls upon, or quickens our tabernacle, our temple, and touches our spirit, our inner man. The Spirit falls, or quickens to anoint,**

strengthen, minister, and empower us for service. When the Spirit of the Living God quickens, or falls heavy upon us, no one can break through and interrupt or disturb God's movement upon our hearts.

The Spirit begins to hover over us like the Spirit of God moved upon the face of the waters in Genesis 1:2. ".... And the Spirit of God moved upon the face of the waters." The Hebrew word for moved is 'rachaph,' pronounced (raw-khaf'). It means that the Spirit began to relax, and hover over the waters. To hover means to remain, or linger in, or near a place. It also means to remain in a stationary position over a place or object.

The Holy Spirit hanged out, or draped Himself over the water, over the tabernacle, and over his people. When the Spirit comes over you, He comes down upon you like a dove descending upon your shoulders. "And the Holy Ghost descended in a bodily shape like a dove upon him, and a voice came from heaven which said, Thou art my beloved Son; in thee I am well pleased." Luke 3:22. When the Spirit moves upon the altars of your heart, He rests upon it. The Spirit begins maneuvering the reins of your heart, whichever way He wills.

The people of every tribe could not enter this secret, holy place. The children could not enter. The priest could not enter. The levites could not enter. Only the high priest had access. All year round, no one entered this room. A heavy veil at its entrance closed the room. No one could enter, or the consequence would have been death! *It was a secret, sanctified, hallowed place!*

It was full of secrecy. The people understood that it was a place where God dwelt. God's presence filled all the room. Every cubic centimeter was filled. Every space held God's presence. This was God's habitat. It was His place of worship, mercy, atonement, oneness, life, and communion. This was a place where only God knew its real richness, and uniqueness.

God operated the Innermost place as to ensure concealment, and to hide it from a sinful people. **IT WAS CONSIDERED AS HOLY GROUND.** The people were not eligible to enter because of their sin. The place was extremely holy. God declared it holy. He pronounced it holy. Sin kept people from the presence of a holy God. The high priest had special qualifications to be eligible to enter on the Day of Atonement. God's immediate presence was sequestered, screened off, secluded, and hidden from view. There-fore, this place remained a secret, and to some a mystery.

### The Secret Place-A Closeness with God

The Innermost Court was known as the place farthermost within the sanctuary. It was a place where the high priest would be closest to God. This place was the secret place. The secret place depicted closeness and a oneness with God. It dealt with being closely re-lated to God in a way in which was close to Him. That closeness with God was related to His character. Primarily, the priest had to be holy, above all. That was God's number one objective. I Peter 1:16 says, "...Be ye holy; for I am holy." *Holiness was God's chief characteristic of His character, therefore, man must have possessed God's holiness to enter in, and commune with Him.* Only the blood consid-ered man holy. Man had to be like God to approach Him. Man had to reflect God's image in a way that made him resemble God through his spirit. Man had to become a reflection of God.

The secret place represented closeness with God, because of the qualities God produced in man's spirit to be like Him. The high priest behaved like God in his spirit, and was chosen by God to represent all the tribes of Israel. The high priest developed close-ness with God. He walked with God. In other words, the high priest became so close to God that he became a friend with God.

If you are a friend of God, then you are close to Him. If you are close to God, you develop intimacy with Him. In developing inti-macy with God, you share personal, intimate, secret things with God. These thoughts in which you share with God can be things in which you have not mentioned to anyone else. These thoughts can be secrets. It is where you are transparent before the Lord, and were the Lord becomes transparent with you.

As you confess your sins to God, and you begin to talk with Him concerning your daily needs, desires, longings, or concerns, He reciprocates your sharing with Him, and He begins to share with you. Wait on God, and listen to Him. This becomes your secret place: your sharing, your talking, your confidentiality God gives you, or your being able to express your innermost feelings, and spirit unto the LORD. He responds by not breaking your confi-dence, **but will begin to reveal, and share things about Himself to you.**

God gave Moses the pattern for the tabernacle, but his brother, Aaron, from the family of Levi, entered the tabernacle, and offered sacrifices unto the Lord on his behalf, along with all the people. He remained obedient; therefore, this afforded him entrance into the holiest place of all.

Psalm 25:14 says, "The secret of the LORD is with them that fear him; and he will shew them his covenant." This signifies familiar friendship, or a familiar close relationship. The word secret in this verse is the Hebrew word 'cowd,' pronounced (sode). It means to have a familiar conversation, and that is among familiar friends. This acquaintance develops because of the level of sharing that takes place.

'Cowd' also means to share in counseling, or to share in secret counsel. Lastly, this word secret means to have intimacy with God, that is, familiar conversation, or a deep knitted closeness, or oneness.

After reading this section above, do you have an idea on what the secret place is today?

### The Secret Place – What's the Secret?
"He that dwelleth in the secret place of the most High shall abide under the shadow of the Almighty." Psalm 91:1.

Let's focus in on the secret place. The word 'secret' is the Hebrew word 'cether,' pronounced (say'-ther). This word means a covering, shelter, hiding place, protection, or secrecy. The word secret also means something that is kept hidden from knowledge, view, or something that is concealed. It is operating in a hidden or confidential manner. The word secret also means something not expressed, but that which is inward.

A secret place is a secluded place. A secret place is beyond ordinary understanding. It is a place where some are unauthorized to go.

The secret place is a place kept hidden from others, or known only to oneself, or to a few. Everyone cannot enter the secret place. Access is prohibited to the unsaved, and to some who are saved.

The secret place can be a solitary place; it is also private, and sequestered. The secret place is a place set apart, or cut off from others. It is a place of sanctification. It is a place where you are insulated by God's protection, yet you are rendered free from any external influence! Certain external influences are restricted! You are free! You are in a place of separation from a mixed, influencing world, and culture. You are confined, but you are confined to holiness! You are set away from all others; you are detached, removed, or alone to be with God. You are cut off, and closed off from fleshly attachments.

The secret place is an exalted place in God. It is a high calling of God. It is the place that is not only your destination, but also your destiny! It is an unlimited, boundless, infinite place in God.

It is a secret place because all do not have access to this realm with God. It's a place only for the righteous. "Blessed are the pure in heart: for they shall see God." Matthew 5:8. Only the high priest could enter into the Holy of Holies, and that entrance was once a year. That entrance took a holy high priest, one who had been sanctified for approaching the Holy God. The entrance was only made by the righteous.

The people never saw the inside of the sanctuary. They were denied entrance. It was sin that kept them out of the presence of God. Not even the priest went into the Holiest place of all. It was one man, for one time, for one nation, who entered into the Innermost court. Anyone who tried to enter unauthorized, would be stricken with death.

The secret place was God's most retired, and private part where he abode. This was a place where God was alone with himself. No strangers or family members could intrude. This was a time when God would commune with man. This communion was only done through first the sprinkling of blood to atone sin. Therefore, the first atonement, that is, (a covering for sin), had to be done for God to accept man's approach to Him.

The secret place is abiding where God abides. It is a sacred, righteous, and holy place. The unrighteous have no place there. Dwelling in the secret place is abiding in a sacred place where the presence of God is preeminent. To dwell is to abide, sit, or abode with Him. If you dwell with God, it is choosing to sit with God in the holy place, and communing with Him. It is sitting with Him in that sacred, holy, secret place.

If you dwell in the secret place, you shall abide under His shadow. You will be able to be sheltered, and protected by God. If you dwell with Him, you shall abide with Him. If you abide under the protection, then you have dwelt with Him. To dwell is to remain there in that place. It also means to inhabit that place, to continue and tarry there with God. To dwell is to live in that place. It is illustrated as a place where you are there so much, that you are really married to God. "Be still, and know that I am God: I will be exalted among the heathen, I will be exalted in the earth." Psalm 46:10.

So there is a secret to God's holiness, and that is man's holiness. There is a secret to worshiping God, and that is to worship Him in spirit and in truth. There is a secret of approaching God's presence, and that is the way of holiness.

### Approaching God's Presence

| Man's Make-Up | Tabernacle | Service |
| --- | --- | --- |
| Flesh | Outer Court | Confession, Thanksgiving |
| Soul | Holy Place | Praise |
| Spirit | Holy of Holies | Worship |

Well, what's the secret to enter God's presence: "Be ye holy, for I am holy". I Peter 1:16. "Who shall ascend into the hill of the LORD? Or who shall stand in his holy place? He that hath clean hands, and a pure heart; who hath not lifted up his soul unto vanity, nor sworn deceitfully." Psalm 24:3,4. "Blessed are the pure in heart: for they shall see God." Matthew 5:8.

If you want to dwell in the secret place of the Most High then you must be holy! You will abide under His protection. You will abide under His covering. You will abide under His guardianship!

When you dwell with God and commune with Him, you become like Him. God is holy!

From the tabernacle, to Solomon's temple, to Jesus' incarnation, to the body of the individual person, called to church, to the glorified body—each has a secret place!

### My Hide-Out
"For in the time of trouble **he shall hide me in his pavilion: in the secret of his tabernacle shall he hide me**; he shall set me up

upon a rock. And now shall mine head be lifted up above mine enemies round about me...." Psalm 27: 5, 6a.

Ever been in trouble? Well, in these times of trouble, God will hide you from trouble, and from your enemies! Rest, and trust in the Lord. The Lord is your hiding place when you are in trouble, when you fear, when you do not know what to do, when you are all alone, or when you feel destitute. Try God in these times, you've love Him even more and more.

In the passage above, the word hide is the word 'tsaphan,' pronounced (tsaw-fan'). Its definition is to literally hide from discovery, or to treasure or store up. The word pavilion is the word 'cok,' pronounced (soke). It means a den, booth, tabernacle, or covert, which is a covering, cover, shelter, hideout, or hideaway. The covering operates in a way to ensure complete concealment, and confidentiality from trouble, or from one's enemies. The hideout is to put or keep you out of sight. It's your refuge! It's a covering. It's your secret place! Hide out there!

As you are covered by the Almighty, you are in a resting place. Rest on the couch. Do not worry about anything, because He has everything under control. This is a place of comfort, and peace. Trouble or anything else cannot enter this place in God. Hide out there!

After coming out of this place, you will have the ability to soar above earthly concerns. You will have answers to problems, and will know how to make certain decisions on different issues in which you are involved. Your heart, mind, and spirit will be strengthened. You will be encouraged, and will have courage! You will not be weary. Hide out there!

What an excellent place to go! What an excellent place to dwell, in the pavilion of the LORD, in the secret of his tabernacle. What an excellent resort, and vacation site to dwell, in the pavilion of the Most High, under His shadow.

**Instead of taking a trip to get away, or register to go on a cruise, first check in at the pavilion of God, in His hide-away.** You will come away more refreshed, more strengthened, and more encouraged than ever before. It will be a place of glory, and peace. You will receive relief, and help from that which saddens, or causes hurt, sorrow, pain, or shame! "Come unto me, all ye that labor and are heavy laden, and I will give you rest. Take my yoke upon you, and learn of me; for I am meek and lowly in heart: and ye shall find rest unto your souls. For my yoke is easy, and my burden is light." Matthew 11: 28-30.

You will prosper there, and you will receive healing from the saps of God's healing anointing from His anointed touch, anointed Spirit, anointed ointment, and His anointed words spoken unto you. His words will be spirit and life unto you. You will rise again! You will be enriched, and be made rich! You will receive victory! Your abundance will supercede your enemies.

He will protect you in your growth towards Him! He will endow you with power! God will give you strategies to use for your enemies. He will pour out grace and mercy unto you. Dwell in the resort of the heavenlies!

The resort of the heavenlies is the abode of God. This is God's home, also known as a dwelling place, a home of security, a home of personal interest, and a home of refuge. This place is your sanctuary! In the sanctuary, you will feel secure, and safe. You feel as if no harm can come to you. Abode in the sanctuary of your spirit, the place where you meet God.

In Psalm 27:5, *the secret of his tabernacle* is used to describe God's place of secrecy, shelter, protection, or a place of covering. The word tabernacle is the Hebrew word 'ohel,' pronounced (o' - hel). It is defined as a dwelling, home, habitation, or sacred tent of Jehovah. Don't you want to go there in time of trouble? You will be directly in God's presence, and will receive direct attention from Him.

### The Apple of God's Eye
"Keep me as *the apple of the eye*, hide me **under the shadow of thy wings**...." Psalm 17:8.

The apple of God's eye is known as His way of saying, "I AM forever watching you! I AM forever seeing you. I AM keeping my eye on YOU! I am watching over you. I AM your watchman, your body guard, your security system, your mode of protection!"

The apple of God eye means what is dearest to Him. It is defined as that which must have extreme care, and protection. God will handle you with special care, and special abundant love. That's sweet care, sweet love!

The apple of God's eye is in the Hebrew custom known as the 'daughter of the eye.' The eye of the body is very delicate, and precious. The eye is more precious, and tender than any other part of the body. Projecting bones protects the eye. It is in a well-protected area of the body. Eyelids, eyelashes, and eyebrows protect the eye. In this case, the eye is well guarded by these other eye parts. The apple of the eye is the pupil of the eye. The eye represents insight, and discernment. You are the apple of God's eye! You are well guarded and protected by His power, and His love.

The pupil is the black circular opening in the center of the iris of the eye, through which light passes to the retina. Notice that it is in the center of the eye itself. This indicates that you are in the center of God's heart, in the core existence of his being. You are the apple of God's eye. This is a secret place!

### YOU are The Apple of God's Eye

### The Secret Closet
"But thou, when thou prayest, enter into thy closet, and when thou hast shut thy door, pray to thy Father which is in secret; and thy Father which seeth in secret shall reward thee openly." Matthew 6:6

The secret closet in Matthew 6:6 is an amazing room! It's a secret room, a secret closet, and a secret place. The word *closet* is the Greek word 'tameion,' pronounced (tam-i'-on). Its meaning is a storage chamber, storeroom, a closet, or a secret room.

Prayer can be held in secret. No one has to know that you are praying. You can offer up silent prayers unto the Lord in secret. As you begin to pray, shut everything out that can serve as a distraction. This has the connotation of going into a room, and shutting the door behind you so that nothing can distract, or disturb you. As you enter into praying to God, you enter into the secret room. It is a secret room, or a secret closet, because no one ever has to know when your entrance is made, what is being said, or heard. It is God who will reward you openly.

Your thoughts are hidden, and God is hidden. No one knows the times that you are in your secret room, unless you tell them, or else they hear you.

My secret room can be my car, a private room on my job, a place within me, or a private place somewhere in my home. The secret closet can be also on a busy street, in a busy home, on a busy job, or in a busy crowd. In other words, you can be anywhere and make entrance into the secret place! The secret place is where you are alone with God, either in mind, thought, or in the spirit. You will always have His undivided attention in the secret room. *"Ask and it shall be given you; seek, and ye shall find; knock and it shall be opened unto you: For every one that asketh receiveth; and he that seeketh findeth; and to him that knocketh it shall be opened."* Matthew 7: 7-8.

Get in your secret room and sup with the Lord. Speak to Him, but do not forget to listen to hear what the Spirit is saying unto your heart.

**The Secret Place-Where You Experience Intimacy, Closeness, Oneness, and is Personal with God.**

*The glory of worship is going from glory
to glory via intimacy with God.*

*Worship is our way into the heart of God.*

*Worship is love.*

# CHAPTER EIGHTEEN

# INTIMACY WITH GOD

"Draw nigh to God, and he will draw nigh to you."  James 4:8
"Abide in me, and I in you."  John 15:4

### What is Intimacy with God?

Intimacy with God is an essential, vital part of our relationship, and fellowship with Him.  To be intimate with God is to possess closeness or oneness with Him.  To be close to God is to be near Him in our relationship with Him.  It is having little or no space between you and God.  When you are close to God, and intimate with Him, eventually the closeness will produce a greater oneness. This oneness will cause you to look more and more like Him!  You will become a reflection, of who God is.

When you are intimate with God, you are constantly thinking, or meditating about Him.  You talk about Him in whatever you do. You acknowledge Him in all your ways.  You delight in Him.  You realize that you cannot do anything without Him. ".... For without me ye can do nothing." John 15:5. "For thou shalt worship no other god: for the LORD, whose name is **JEALOUS**, is a jealous God." Exodus 34:14.

Intimacy is rooted in the deep, innermost place inside man. It's that private space within us. A person would have to be closely related to you, or very close to you in order for you to experience intimacy. **Sex is not a substitute for intimacy.**

Intimacy must take place between you and God. You must be close to Him in order to experience His royal intimacy! "Draw nigh to me, and I will draw nigh to you." James 4:8. This verse is in the *imperative* command. This verse is conditional. If you draw nigh to the Father, He will draw nigh to you. That's a guarantee! His word will not return unto Him void! To draw nigh means to be near, or close to Him. To draw nigh is the Greek word, *"eggizo"*. This term also means to closely approach Him. To draw nigh to God is to long for Him, or to thirst for Him. It means to desire Him. To be intimate with God is to put your whole heart into the relationship. "And ye shall seek me, and find me, when ye shall **search for me** with **all** your heart." Jeremiah 29:13.

*To search for God* is to follow Him and obey Him. It also means to ask of Him, or to consult with Him. To search for God also means to seek Him in prayer and in worship.

In giving God your whole heart, whoever that you love dearest, must be offered to God, that God might possess your whole heart! Abraham had to offer his son Isaac unto God, because God wanted all of Abraham's heart. "Thou shalt love the Lord thy God with all thy heart, and with all thy soul, and with all thy strength, and with all thy mind; and thy neighbor as thyself." Luke 10:27.

Being intimate with another is being attached by mutual interests, affections, desires, or love. Intimacy with God is being one-on-one with Him, without any intrusions. It's a personal thing! It's a private thing!

Intimacy involves people whom you trust, and love! You cherish them! You adore them! You honor them! You are sensitive to their needs, desires, longings, and wants! It's a person so close to you, that secrets are shared, especially, shortcomings, fears, and secret sins, with extreme confidentiality. (Isn't this just like God?) These things are shared for inner healing, and repentance!

### God's Intimate Name, "ABBA Father"

Being intimate is sharing a heart-to-heart, interactive relationship with the Father. We address Him intimately, as a child to his earthly father, as "ABBA FATHER". ".... But ye have received the Spirit of adoption, whereby we cry, Abba, Father." Romans 8:15.

Notice the phrase is not *"my"* or *"our" Father, as in Judaism, or as in the Lord's Prayer,"* but 'ABBA FATHER.' It can help to know the Father more intimately, by merely knowing His names.

God's intimate name is wrapped up in His name 'Father'. In fact, all of God's names are wrapped up in his name, "FATHER!" Heavenly Father, Abba Father, our Father, my Father, everlasting Father, merciful Father, all render a closeness to the Father. Jesus revealed a loving, intimate relationship with His father by calling Him, FATHER. By calling His Father, *Abba* it revealed an intimate, close relationship, unlike that of any other. Jesus said, "...Abba, Father," claiming His sonship was very unique. Abba suggests dearness, intimacy, love, and extreme care. God is greater than our human fathers are. He's awesomely far beyond human attributes of that of a father that one could ever imagine, dream, or hope for!

**"Abba" (ab-ba) means head of the family.** Abba insinuates unreasoning trust. It can mean grandfather, founding father, ancestor, founder of a lifestyle, or occupation. For instance, Abraham, *"Ab-raham"* means 'Father of many nations.' Father means a parent signifying a nourisher, or protector. Abba is equivalent to our English words, 'papa', or 'daddy.' It is a name in which we look to God for faithful provision, and protection. It's a name of trust and is based upon a personal intimate love relationship.

A very close association, contact, or familiarity marks intimacy. The association is so closely knitted that the product of this closeness is a development of a very warm friendship. The friendship develops through being in a long-term association with the Father. It takes time for relationships to become intimate!

Intimacy is the deepest nature of an individual. It is located in the innermost place in a person's being, and heart. It is inwardly on the inside of one's heart. Intimacy can sometimes be very hard to develop, if the individual refuses to let you into their innermost places of their heart. In this case, fear, or sometimes even hatred, controls the opening, or closing of that person's heart so that no one can enter.

Being intimate with God is to be so close to him that you begin to look, act, walk, talk, live, and become just like him.

### Unconditional Love, Intimacy's Foundation & Power

The underlying foundation and power of intimacy is **unconditional love**. *Expressing unconditional love to your partner is the driving key, or driving power in reaching ultimate peaks in intimacy.*

In intimacy, love that is unconditional is a dimension of love that knows no limits! It is a love that has no strings attached. This *superior, royal, rich, exquisite* type of love is without any conditions; it knows no boundaries. This type of love is **agape** love, that which comes from God, and is produced, or birthed by Him.

Unconditional love has **no reservations**. It is without hesitation. There is no doubt that it's there, and it is there without question. It is unreserved! Unconditional love is given away *wholeheartedly*, and is very *genuine*. It **is given** away freely, **without any force, or obligation**, whatsoever.

You do not have to ask for unconditional love; it's always there! You do not have to wonder whether you are loved. God loves you. This love is for you; only receive it! It's yours! This is love from God's own heart. This love is intimacy's foundation. It is intimacy's strength, and its power.

Unconditional love is **absolute**. This means that this love is: complete, perfect in quality or nature, faultless, flawless, pure, and of course, **unadulterated!**

Unconditional love is the ultimate type of love of our thought, and being. It is **independent** in and of itself. There is no other type of love like this dimension of love. You cannot compare it to or with any other type of love. It is matchless. It is in a category all by itself.

Unconditional love is **unselfish**, and it gives. It gives until it cannot give any more. Unconditional love gives its very best. It does not give anything less than the best. "For God so loved the world that He **gave** His **only begotten** Son, that whosoever believeth in Him shall not perish, but have everlasting life." St. John 3:16. God gave. God gave his absolute, very best! God gave the world love. God gave His only Son!

Unconditional love is a very **mature** type of love. Only the mature type of Christian can exhibit it, in all its fullness. When all

other types of love (*Eros, Phileo, Storge*) fail, or fall short, unconditional love (agape) keeps going on, and on, and on.

Unconditional love does not worry what others think. **It loves
in spite of....** It's **supremely excellent in quality. Unconditional
love never fails.**

It is **love that is spiritual, and not sexual.** It is not a fleshly
type of love, but is spiritual. All christians possess this kind of love
within them. Some have hard times, or complications allowing this
love to shine through, being exemplary of the Father's love. **This
love is unknown to the world. The world holds grudges, remembers your faults and shortcomings, and is selfish. The world does
not have the power to express love that knows no boundaries.**

**Unconditional love gives intimacy substance.** Without love,
intimacy is empty! Intimacy promotes closeness, and nearness. If
there were no love, how would you become close? How would you
become that reflection of who God really is?

What this type of love does is that it still loves even after you
fall short of God's glory! "For all have sinned, and fallen short of
the glory of God". Romans 3:23. Unconditional love will love even
after your faults are displayed. Your mistakes, errors, secret sins,
shortcomings, or any type of sins cannot stop the flow of unconditional love. This is true, because there is grace within the love;
there is mercy within this type of love. Forgiveness keeps you together. "Where sin did abound, grace did much more abound."
Romans 5:20. **THERE IS NO GREATER LOVE!**

### Intimacy in the Marriage Union

What do you think a marriage would be like if there was **no**
intimacy? **That marriage or union would eventually die!** It will
wither away, like the green grass. It will be carried off into the
**atmosphere and be no more. Marriage was designed for intimacy
to flow. God ordained marriage to display degrees of intimacy!
DO NOT TRY MARRIAGE WITHOUT INCLUDING INTIMACY!
YOU WILL DEFEAT ONE OF MARRIAGE'S PURPOSES!**

The marriage relationship that has been ordained by God must
not lack unconditional love. Marriage is the ultimate relationship
on this earth that brings about the closes intimacy between two
people. There is no greater relationship on earth between two people
that can promote a greater closeness. **The closest you can get to**

any person on earth is not with your friend, relative, or family member, but in the marriage union!

The marriage union is the greatest union of two people on this earth. You may be thinking about that relationship either between: a mother and son, mother and daughter, father and son, father and daughter, friend and friend, relative and relative, aunt and niece, aunt and nephew, uncle and niece or nephew, or one with grandparents. The bottom line is that the marriage relationship is above all of these. **Two human beings are the closest in a marriage relationship.** You may be close to that son, daughter, friend, or love one, **but** it is not as close as you can be with a spouse! All relationships have their ultimate peak. **Marriage surpasses them all.**

Some may even be thinking about the **world's system** today. You may be thinking about that relationship that is between two men, or either two women. **The world paints a beautiful love scene between homosexuals, or lesbians; however, and but.... God says it is SIN! You cannot be comfortable, nor have absolute peace living in SIN! "There is no peace, saith God, to the wicked." Isaiah 57:21.**

You cannot be comfortable and be at peace with yourself, or with God, when you are living in opposition to the law of God, the word of God, and the commandment of God. You cannot be at peace, and bluntly defy God, His nature, His character, His order, and pattern for living. *God made Adam and Eve, not Adam and Steve, or Edith and Eve!*

He made man and woman to be one flesh, not man, and man, or woman and woman. **I rebuke these thoughts, systems, lifestyles, practices, philosophies, and ideologies in the name of Jesus!** He had **no intention** of two men lying together, or two women lying together. If this fits you, **REPENT!** Turn to Jesus!

Just like their can be false prophets, false teachers, false pastors, false apostles, and false evangelists; there can also be false relationships. These are counterfeit! They are counterfeit of the real relationship.

Therefore, in the marriage relationship, there must be intimacy. It cannot stand without it. IT CANNOT BE WHAT GOD ORDAINED IT TO BE WITHOUT IT. You must be able to love in spite of your spouse's errors, mistakes, shortcomings, secret faults, and sins! You must love your spouse without any limitations; love them unconditional. LOVE COVERS A MULTITUDE OF SIN!

The more and more you love your spouse with expressions of unconditional love; the more and more intimacy will **continually produce itself.** You will become closer and closer to your spouse. Deep rooted feelings will surface more and more. Sharing will be at its peak. You will be able to share feelings, and concerns from your **innermost** place, and your spouse will not turn from you. Forgiveness will always be in order.

When you truly forgive someone, eventually you will forget it! God does us the same way. We first don't ask for forgiveness, but we confess our sins, then God is faithful and just to forgive us of our sins, and cleanse us from all unrighteousness. I John 1: 9. God forgives us, and then He remembers our sins no more. That's the power mode of forgiveness—TO FORGET, TO REMEMBER NO MORE! God's forgiveness is so powerful that He forgets our sin. God's forgiveness is so powerful that He remembers them no more. God's forgiveness is so powerful that He forgives us seventy times seven —and that's infinitely. THIS DOES NOT GIVE YOU A LICENSE TO SIN!

So, just like the marriage union (which is exemplary of God's union with Himself, i.e., Father, Son, and Holy Ghost) cannot live without intimacy; then likewise, our fellowship with the Father.

Get to know God intimately. Come into a new awareness of His awesome love for us. When you realize this awesome love that God has for you, then and only then, will your intimacy with Him heighten, widen, and deepen to levels unknown. God marvelously and amazingly loves you! He demonstrated this love by giving His only begotten Son.

As you come into a fresh revelation of God's love, then you will begin to love God unconditionally. You will except His will without reservations. You will not have limits for how much God loves you. You will realize that all things work together for good, to them that love God and are called according to His purpose. Romans 8:28. God may reveal certain things about you to you. Receive His analysis. Ask Him to search your heart, When He reveals these things to you about yourself, this is an expression of intimacy. It's intimacy because it's personal.

If He asks you to alter, or change a part of your character, do so. This would be expresses His love for you. Whom He loves He rebukes and chastens. **Be a hearer of the word and not a doer only. This would deceive you if you were only a doer.**

**Your character** is important to God. Your **character is** a combination of qualities, traits, gifts, talents, or abilities that distinguishes you from another. Your character is your moral, ethical, or spiritual strength. Character is the thing that causes you to be competent in certain areas. Your character is your reputation, and can be sometimes viewed as the public's estimation, or opinion of you. Your character is a portrait of who you really are.

Who are you behind a closed door? Who are you when you think that no one's looking? Who are you when you are out of the saints' view, or not in church? Who are you when you are being mistreated, abused, and talked about? Who are you in the dark? Who are you when you are all alone? Who are you? Are you that same person when everyone is looking at you?

**Your character** is your behavior. Your character is how people identify or describe you. It is how people mark you; it's your traits. Your character is how peculiar you are. It includes your dignity, integrity, and principles. It is knowing how much people can depend on you. Your character is your name; or the opinions one gives of you.

Your character is the sum total of your emotional, intellectual, moral, worldly and spiritual make-up. It's your complexion, disposition, and your nature.

God's character includes His attributes, and His glory. His glory is the sum total of all He is. God says, "I AM!"

The reason why God wants to work character within you **is that you are heading into your destiny.** Your destiny is the place where God will use you.

When God leads you into that greater realm of your destiny, your character must be in tact. You see, that is why you need to be intimate with God. He will polish, and refine you. It's for your greater place of destiny. You want to know deep rooted, embedded faults, and hang ups, because if these things are not slain, they will be the very things that will pull you down in your time to come.

### Intimacy with God is to Know Him

"**That I may know him,** and the power of his resurrection, and the fellowship of his sufferings, being made conformable unto his death..." Philippians 3:10.

Get to know Jesus! If you were interested in a person, the first thing you would do is to get to know that person. There would be no full relationship, without first getting to know the other person.

In Philippians 3:10, the word know is the Greek word '**ginosko**,' pronounced (ghin-oce'-ko). Ginosko means to learn, or to know a person. This word is further defined as to come into an understanding of a person to the extent that you begin to know, and discern how they think, or feel. To know means to become acquainted with.

When Paul stated that he wanted to know Jesus, he was implying that he wanted to know Jesus on grounds of a personal encounter, or experience. **To know** also gives the connotation of being able to see spiritually with a clear mental perception of who Jesus is. To know is to have spiritual insight, or to be able to discover new aspects, and characteristics of a person.

In this connotation, to know one is to pay attention to them, and observe their movement. This is like observing what God is doing in the earth, to see Him act. It's examining, and inspecting His every move.

To know Him is to turn your eyes, mind, and your complete attention to Him. IT'S BEING SO ATTENTIVE TO JESUS THAT YOU BEGIN TO KNOW HIS LIKES, AND DISLIKES.

TO GET TO KNOW GOD is visiting Him repeatedly. You must.... Be still and KNOW that He is God. You must sit down, and dwell in God's presence. You must abide with Him. You must sit, and join yourselves together with one mind, and one heart. It is cherishing who Jesus is.

Sit down; learn His ways! Know what He loves; know what He hates! Learn what pleases Him. "Without faith it is impossible to please Him, for he that cometh to God must believe that He is, and is a rewarder of them that diligently seek Him." Be intimate with God.

*Worship Him with all your heart, mind, soul, strength, and might.*

*Worship is fireworks exploding into the heavens unto our Father.*

# CHAPTER NINETEEN

## COMMUNION WITH GOD

" *And thou shalt make a mercy seat of pure gold: two cubits and a half shall be the length thereof, and a cubit and a half the breadth thereof. And thou shalt make two cherubims of gold, of beaten work shalt thou make them, in the two ends of the mercy seat. And make on cherub on the one end, and the other cherub on the other end: even of the mercy seat shall ye make the cherubims on the two ends thereof. And the cherubims shall stretch forth their wings on high, covering the mercy seat with their wings, and their faces shall look one to another; toward the mercy seat shall the faces of the cherubims be. And thou shalt put the mercy seat above upon the ark; and in the ark thou shalt put the testimony that I shall give thee. **And there I will meet with thee, and I will commune with thee from above the mercy seat, from between the two cherubims which are upon the ark of the testimony, of all things which I will give thee in commandment unto the children of Israel.**" Exodus 25: 17-22.

It is my heart's desire to daily, and intensely commune with the Father. You may equate prayer with communion; however, communion runs deeper than prayer, because of the close two-way involvement. Prayer is man talking to God. Communion is talking, loving, fellowshipping, communicating, and intimately sharing with God, and God sharing with man. Thus, communing involves God responding to us, as well as, man responding to Him through intimately sharing, and communicating. If we hear no voice from God at the first moment of approaching him, we ought not to be satisfied unless, while we are speaking to God, God speaks to us. "Unto thee will I cry, O LORD my rock; be not silent to me: lest, if thou be silent to me, I become like them that go down into the pit." Psalm 28:1.

Communion, with the Father, is a state of intimacy with Him. Holy Communion! Sweet Communion! Awesome Communion! Peaceful Communion! It is a heightened place in God. I noticed that God allowed man not to commune with him, if man was not holy. The same is true today. We cannot approach the throne of God unless there is repentance, confession of sins, and God's willing desire to forgive and extend mercy unto His people. We cannot commune with God unless we have accepted Jesus Christ as our personal Savior.

In order to **commune**, there must be something in **common**. There must be a bond, or tie which unite one to the other. There must be a link. You must be in God's family to commune with Him. Jesus Christ is our link to the Father. We have a binding agreement, or covenant which no man can put asunder. Jesus is our bond.

First, let's look at the definitions of communion. Communion is an exalted, high state of worship. It is a state of intimacy, which is heightened by one's sensitivity, and receptivity. You become completely sensitive to God as you commune with Him. You long to hear His voice. You know that He is present. You are aware of His presence to the extent that you feel His touch. You sense His presence. You know that God is there with you. You praise Him. You sing to Him. You begin to speak in your spiritual language unto Him. You worship, worship, and worship Him. You bow before Him. You lie prostrate before Him. **You wait in silence for Him to** manifest Himself to you in your presence. Finally, with a still, soft, audible yet silent voice, He speaks.

After you hear Him speak to your heart, you respond. The communication becomes informal, yet revealing from both sides. You reveal the hidden secrets of your heart, and He begins to reveal Himself to you like you have never known. You must come before God's presence in humility with an attitude of honesty when you begin to share. You share so that you can know Him personally, and intimately. You also share in order to meet yours and His needs.

When you commune, you lay all of you before each another. The more you become transparent before the other, the greater the intimacy will be. When you commune, it is a must that both sides participate. One side cannot do all of the talking; neither can one side do all of the listening. When God communes with man, He sometimes make Himself known through revelations, visions, dreams, prophetic speaking, or through His written word.

To commune literally means to speak with another. When you speak with another in communing, by definition of the word itself, you take turns communicating with each other. When you commune, you meet in order to deliberate together, or compare and share views. This action of communing must be unhurried. You talk with the Lord, carefully, and slowly thinking about a decision to be made.

One reason for conferring with the Father, is to help you make right decisions, and for your paths to be directed. Since you are communing with the Lord, then you can be casual, and very informal in your communion with Him. This type of communion with the Lord will take time. You must learn how to sit silently, awaiting a response from Him. You must be attentive, and be keen to listening for the still, quiet voice of God.

In the Greek sense of the definition, communion is the word 'koinonia,' pronounced (koy-nohn-ee'-ah). This Greek word is the same word used for the word 'fellowship.' Its definition means to have fellowship with enjoyment, to have association with, joint participation with, or to have intercourse. Understand that communion is a level of being intimate. The word 'koinonia' is also defined as a gift jointly contributed, and proof of one's fellowship with another.

Communion is communicating. It is communicating intimately with each other. Communion transcends prayer. Communion is deeper than prayer.

In order to commune with one another, you must be that other party's friend, comrade, or companion in some way. In being partners, a special sharing takes place. This sharing should be concerning anything from the heart of either partner, like common experiences, desires, and interests of the two.

The communion between the two begins to further develop with the sharing of intimate, hidden, innermost, and sometimes unspeakable thoughts of the heart. The sharing begins to go to other levels, revealing the character of each person. In most cases, the untapped, hidden, qualities are uncovered, or revealed. There is a sharing and participation in the sufferings of Christ. "That I may know him, and the power of the resurrection, and the fellowship of his sufferings, being made conformable unto his death;...." Philippians 3:10.

The Hebrew form of commune is the word 'dabar,' pronounced (daw-bar'). It means to either speak, declare, converse, command, promise, warn, threaten, sing, meditate, or to talk with one another. Notice, the word also carries as its definition, to promise another.

### The Meeting Place
In Exodus 25:22, ....

*"And there I will meet with thee, and I will commune with thee from above the mercy seat, from between the two cherubims which are upon the ark of the testimony, of all things which I will give thee in commandment unto the children of Israel," God said that He would meet with man and commune with him from above the mercy seat.* This meeting spot is the appearance of God in His regal state upon His throne of glory and mercy. The mercy seat was in the Holy of Holies. The Holy of Holies was in the Innermost Court of the tabernacle of Moses, or the meeting tent. The Holy of Holies was symbolic of the heaven of heavens [heaven itself, the supreme heaven], or the third heaven, where God abode [the palace or kingdom of God]. The Holy of Holies is a place of worship, and reverence to God. It is the place within man that is known as the inner man. The Holy of Holies was a place of worship because it was where God dwelt. It was a place where you could approach God's pres-

ence, and His throne. The Holy of Holies was a place of justice, yet mercy intervened by the sprinkling of the symbolic blood of the Lamb.

In Exodus 30:36, "And thou shalt beat some of it very small, and put of it before the testimony in the tabernacle of the congregation, where I will meet with thee: it shall be unto you most holy," announces that the meeting will be most holy to those who enter in and commune.

"And the LORD said unto Moses, Speak unto Aaron thy brother, that he come not at all times into the holy place within the vail before the mercy seat, which is upon the ark; that he die not: for I will appear in the cloud upon the mercy seat." Leviticus 16:2.

"And when Moses was gone into the tabernacle of the congregation to speak with him, then he heard the voice of one speaking unto him from off the mercy seat that was upon the ark of testimony, from between the two cherubims: and he spake unto him." Numbers 7:89.

"The LORD reigneth; let the people tremble: he sitteth between the cherubims; let the earth be moved." Psalm 99:1.

In Exodus 25:22, there is an evident allusion to the oracle of the mercy seat, called the speaking place.

In Exodus 25, God's communion with His people signified a divine distance from man. This holy approach to God represented God's nature. Only the holy could approach God and that approach could only be made with a blood offering. Only the high priest could enter the Holy of Holies and approach God. The priests, levites, and the common people were not allowed into the Innermost Court. Sin kept them out. The high priest represented Jesus Christ, with his precious blood, and his perfection—without spot, blemish, or any wrinkles. The distance from God represented barriers which were not yet removed between God, and man. It also stood for drawbacks in perfectly communing with God. The veil represented a closed door to man, that the way had not yet been made for man's entrance.

Today, man have found entrance into God's presence through repentance, salvation, redemption, sanctification, thanksgiving, holiness; and through praise and worship. Psalm 100:2, 4 says "....Come before His presence with singing....Enter into His gates with thanksgiving, and into His courts with praise." Still today, in order to approach God, steps must be taken in holiness towards him. For it is only the pure in heart, that will see God.

### The Impossible Communion: Communion Forbidden

"Be ye not unequally yoked together with unbelievers: for what fellowship hath righteousness with unrighteousness? and what communion hath light with darkness? And what concord hath Christ with Belial? or what part hath he that believeth with an infidel? And what agreement hath the temple of God with idols? for ye are the temple of the living God; as God hath said, I will dwell in them, and walk in [them]; and I will be their God, and they shall be my people. Wherefore come out from among them, and be ye separate, saith the Lord, and touch not the unclean [thing]; and I will receive you, And will be a Father unto you, and ye shall be my sons and daughters, saith the Lord Almighty." II Corinthians 6:14-18.

'That which we have seen and heard declare we unto you, that ye also may have fellowship with us: and truly our fellowship is with the Father, and with his Son Jesus Christ....If we say that we have fellowship with him, and walk in darkness, we lie, and do not the truth: But if we walk in the light, as he is in the light, we have fellowship one with another, and the blood of Jesus Christ his Son cleanseth us from all sin." I John 1:3, 6-7.

Communion, or fellowship is forbidden between the believer with the unbeliever; the righteous with the unrighteous; light with darkness; Christ with Belial; believer with an infidel; or the temple of God with idols. The two do not mix; they do not agree. They do not have anything in common. "How can two walk together, except they be agreed?" Amos 3:3.

It is impossible for light and darkness to have any fellowship. In I John 1: 6, God is saying that if you say that you have fellowship, or communion with Him; and on the contrary, you are steadily walking in darkness, you are lying—and the truth is not in you. Therefore, if you are in communion with God, you will walk in the light. Verse 5 says that God is light, and in Him is no darkness at all. If you are having fellowship with God, you are therefore walking in the light. If you are not in communion with God, then you are walking in darkness. To walk in the light is to walk in truth.

"Hear, O my people, and I will admonish you! O Israel, if you will listen to Me! There shall be no foreign god among you; nor shall you worship any foreign god. I am the Lord your God, who brought you out of the land of Egypt; open your mouth wide, and I will fill it. But my people would not heed my voice, and Israel would have none of Me. So I gave them over to their own stubborn heart, to walk in their own counsels. Oh, that my people would listen to me, that Israel would walk in my ways! I would soon subdue their enemies, and turn my hand against their adversaries." Psalm 81:8-14.

In this passage of scripture, God is pleading for the nation of Israel to listen to Him. God pleaded for them to hear His voice. We should ask the Lord has He been trying to tell me something that I desperately needed to hear? How many times has God spoken to me, and I was doing my own thing, and did not hear His voice? How many times have you communed with other foreign people, when God was divinely beckoning you into His presence? Selah!

Our schedules can be filled with good works; however, God can obviously be left out. My most valuable lesson in communing with God is to learn how to listen to Him. God's voice is waiting to be heard! When you hear the voice of God through communing with Him, you can then launch into the greatest, most awesome tasks ever imagined. If we are tuned to the wrong voice, then whatever we do in terms of assignments, or duties; will not be of our greatest. Our greatest success is found through listening and hearing the voice of God, and not the voice of man. This indicates an importance in communing with the Father. God desires to commune with you.

You cannot commune with the world and God. "No man can serve two masters: for either he will hate the one, and love the other; or else he will hold to the one, and despise the other. Ye cannot serve God and mammon." Matthew 6:24. "...Know ye not that the friendship of the world is enmity with God? whosoever therefore will be a friend of the world is the enemy of God." James 4:4. The unbeliever is absolutely incapable of understanding the things of God anyway. "But the natural man receiveth not the things of the Spirit of God: for they are foolishness unto him: neither can he know them, because they are spiritually discerned." 1 Corinthians 2:14.

God desires you to commune with Him. The problem we have is that we want to commune with darkness, and unrighteousness, which will cut off our communion with the Father. **Because of the intimacy that communion produces, be careful who you commune with!** You become like the person you commune with! The two of you become one! You will develop one mind, one heart, and one strength that no one can put asunder!

### God's Goals in Communing With His People

One goal that God has in mind in communing with Him is that we may comprehend the truth. He wants us to know the truth. "And ye shall know the truth, and the truth shall make you free." John 8:32. God wants us to understand what He is saying. He wants to lead, guide, direct, and instruct you. He wants you to have life more abundantly. He wants you to reach your destiny in Him. Therefore, if we do not hear Him, or if we cannot hear His voice, then there is something in our lives that hinders a clear path of communication.

The Father wants us to know the truth about Himself. He wants us to have more than a head knowledge of Him, but He wants us to have a heart knowledge of Him. He wants us to experience His joy, His holiness, His power, His love, His mercy, His grace, His richness, His kindness, His majesty, His presence and communion with Him. I must know him! Remember, this is your greatest aim! We must be able to say: 'I know Him'. I can say I know Him as a smiting stone against my enemies, a healer of broken hearts, a healer of pain, a forerunner into my tomorrows, a Bishop of my soul and finances, a revealer the secrets of my heart, the Amen of decisions in my life, a channel of new mercies each day, an overseer of choices in life, a provider, comforter and lover, a shield against wickedness, a battle ax unto my enemies, or a mighty fortress against diseases, illnesses, poverty, temptation, fiery darts of the enemy, or against slick impostors!

We need to know Him, and know the truth about Him, because in knowing Him, we find out better who we are in Him, because we are in Him and are made in His image. For example, God is faithful {Deut. 7:9, I Cor. 1:9}, and He says to me—be thou faithful unto death{Rev. 2:10}; God is holy {Psa. 99:5, 99:9}, and He says to me—be thou holy for I am holy{I Pet. 1:16}; God is love {I John 4:7,8}, and He says to me—love the Lord thy God with all thy soul, mind, heart, and strength, and love thy neighbor as you love yourself {Luke 10:27}; God is mighty {Deut. 7:21}—He says to me, give unto the Lord, O ye mighty {Psa. 29:1}; Jesus is King and High Priest{Matt. 27:37, John 18:37, Heb. 4:14, Heb. 6:20}—He says to me behold, I make you kings, and priests unto me{Rev. 1:6, 5:10}; God is omnipotent{Matt. 28:18}—He says to me, I give you power over the wicked one{Luke 10:19}; God is a healer{Ex. 15:26}—He says to me, and ye shall lay your hands on the sick, and they shall recover{Mark 16:18}; Jesus is the Good Shepherd{John 10:11,14}—He says to me, Feed my sheep{John 21:16, 17}; God is one{Deut. 6:4, Mark 12:29, Gal. 3: 20}—He says to me, that you may be one{John 17:21-23}; or God is light{I John 1:5, Rev. 21:23}—He says to me, let your light shine before men{Matt. 5:16}. Seek communion with God.

# Communion with God

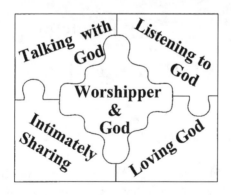

## The Components for Having Communion with God

*Worship given unto the Father is love to our Bridegroom,*
*Lover, Sweetheart, and our Beloved Husband.*

*Surgery repairs incisions to the body.*
*Worship repairs incisions to the spirit.*

*Worship is medicine to your body, soul, and spirit.*

# CHAPTER TWENTY

# LOST COMMUNION
# WITH THE FATHER

### The Story of the Prodigal Son

" **A** nd he said, A certain man had two sons: And the younger of them said to *his* father, Father, give me the portion of goods that falleth *to me*. And he divided unto them *his* living. And not many days after the younger son gathered all together, and took his journey into a far country, and there wasted his substance with riotous living. And when he had spent all, there arose a mighty famine in that land; and he began to be in want. And he went and joined himself to a citizen of that country; and he sent him into his fields to feed swine. And he would fain have filled his belly with the husks that the swine did eat: and no man gave unto him. And when he came to himself, he said, How many hired servants of my father's have bread enough and to spare, and I perish with hunger! I will arise and go to my father, and will say unto him, Father, I have sinned against heaven, and before thee, And am no more worthy to be called thy son: make me as one of thy hired servants. And he arose, and came to his father. But when he was yet a great way off, his father saw him, and had compassion, and ran, and fell on his neck, and kissed him. And the son said unto him, Father, I have sinned against heaven, and in thy sight, and am no more worthy to be called thy son. But the father said to his servants, Bring forth the best robe, and put *it* on him; and put a ring on his hand, and shoes on *his* feet: And bring hither the fatted calf, and kill *it*; and let us eat, and be merry: For this my son was dead, and is alive again; he was lost, and is found. Luke 15:11-32.

This father and son lost their communion with each other. The son left the Father. It was joy to the Father to commune with His children. The sons loved the communion with the Father, and the Father loved the communion with the sons. But now, worship was gone.

"Father, I will that they also, whom thou hast given me, **be with me where I am**; that they may behold my glory, which thou hast given me: for thou lovedst me before the foundation of the world." John 17:24.

"Thou wilt shew me the path of life: in thy presence *is* **fulness of joy**; at thy right hand *there are* pleasures for evermore." Psalm 16:11.

The son enjoyed being in the Father's presence. The home of the Father represents a place in God. It was a certain place. It was a place of harmony, and oneness. They were one, and inseparable. Nothing could put their relationship asunder. The love was too great! Then could anything separate the son from the Father's love?

"Who shall separate us from the love of Christ? *shall* tribulation, or **distress, or persecution**, or famine, or nakedness, or peril, or sword? As it is written, For thy sake we are killed all the day long; we are accounted as sheep for the slaughter. Nay, in all these things we are more than conquerors through him that loved us. For I am persuaded, that neither death, nor life, nor angels, nor principalities, nor powers, nor things present, nor things to come,...Nor height, nor depth, nor any other creature, shall be able to separate us from the love of God, which is in Christ Jesus our Lord." Romans 8:35-39.

How could it have happened? Why did the son leave? Did not the son sense, and know that the Father was in love with him? Could the son see his Father's heart? Could the son see that the Father loved the communion between the two of them? Could the son feel the heartbeat of the Father? Could the son sense in his spirit that he was in the best place? Did the son have insight to know, and feel the passionate love from the Father's heart?

How did the Father feel when his son left Him? What was the condition of the Father's heart when the son came and asked for his premature inheritance? How did the Father feel knowing that the son no longer wanted to commune with Him? Why would such joy that they had experienced, each day all of a sudden not be the fulness of joy to the son? Why did the son seek elsewhere?

Did the son know that whatever the Father had belonged to him also? Did the Father communicate through communing with the son that what He had belonged to him too? Did the son know that the Father was rich? Did the son know the extent of His Father's love for him? Did the Father show love to the son? Was it overwhelming?

Did the son know that when he left that he would come back someday, even though he said he would not? What led the son back home? What led the son back to the Father? What led the son back in communion with the Father? What led the son back in oneness with the Father? What led the son to inherit what he never seemed to think that he had when he returned? Did the Father give up on the son?

Did the Father each day long for the return of the son? Did anyone understand the heart of the Father? Did the son know that the Father watched for him each day? Did the Father show faith in the return of His son? What was the son's turning point? Did the son have to experience lack? Did the son have to experience pain? Did the son have to experience life in the pig's pen? Did the son have to come to nothing? Did the son have to come to nothing just to see, and know His Father's love?

Was the Father's heart broken? Did the Father long to commune with His son? Did the son miss communion with the Father? Did the son find anyone else to commune with like he had done with his Father? Did the son see the value of the Father's love, and His communion? Could it have been that all this happened for the son to see the everlasting love of the Father? Did the son come back with a contrite heart? Did the son come back with a heart of repentance? Was the son sorry that he ever separated himself from his Father?

God sits, waiting, longing for his sons to come back and commune with Him. Draw nigh unto God, and He will draw nigh unto you. He's waiting on you. Come back and experience that fulness of joy you once experienced. Come back into fellowship with the Father. Come back home.

You see, in the Father's presence is fulness of joy. The fulness of joy is a season of apparently inexhaustible happiness. It is a place of wealth, richness, happiness, comfort, support, peace, harmony, joy, and extreme love generating from the Father. It is a place of harvest, and bliss. Peace is the order of this place. Righteous living was its vine. It is a place of an influx of warmth, love, compassion, passion, affection, kindness, lovingkindness, and not just mercy, but tender mercy.

Nothing can separate us from the Father's love. "Who shall separate us from the love of Christ? *shall* tribulation, or **distress, or persecution**, or famine, or nakedness, or peril, or sword? As it is written, For thy sake we are killed all the day long; we are accounted as sheep for the slaughter. Nay, in all these things we are more than conquerors through him that loved us. For I am persuaded, that neither death, nor life, nor angels, nor principalities, nor powers, nor things present, nor things to come...Nor height, nor depth, nor any other creature, shall be able to separate us from the love of God, which is in Christ Jesus our Lord." Romans 8:35-39.

Who or what can separate me from the Father's love...........nothing, or no one!!!!!!!!!

Commune with the Father. The Father seeks communion with His sons. We are the sons of God! He is waiting on you! Shalom.

*Worship is the book of Leviticus.*

*The vine is the lifeline to the branches.*
*Worship is the lifeline to the saints.*

*Like thunder that has a language of its own,*
*worship is a sweet language unto God.*

# CHAPTER TWENTY-ONE

# THE SHEKINAH GLORY

" And Moses was not able to enter into the tent of the congregation, because the cloud abode thereon, and the glory of the LORD filled the tabernacle." Exodus 40:35.

"And let them make me a sanctuary; that I may **dwell** among them." Exodus 25:8

Shekinah! Glory! Glory! Glory! Glory! Glory! Glory! Glory! The Glory of God is the presence of God. The presence of God is the face of God. When you say glory, you invoke God's presence! His presence comes and surrounds you. When you shout glory, you invoke God's face! Shekinah! Shekinah! Shekinah!

"Shekinah" is a word that is not found in the Bible, but alluded to in the scriptures. The Shekinah is the glory, or the mighty presence of God dwelling in the midst of His people. In history, the

Shekinah is referenced to God Himself, and to the Holy Spirit. Shekinah reflects the fact that God dwells in His sanctuary (Ex. 25:8), or among His people (Ex. 29:45). In these two verses the word dwell is the Hebrew word "shakan", pronounced (shaw-kan'). "Shakan" means to settle down, abide, dwell, tabernacle, reside, establish, or to lie. The word "Shekinah" is derived from the verb "shakan", which means to dwell. Shekinah is a dwelling glory!

The glory of God is another name for the Shekinah. "And Moses was not able to enter into the tent of the congregation, because the **cloud** abode thereon, and the **glory of the LORD** filled the tabernacle." Exodus 40:35. The word cloud in this verse is the Hebrew word "`anan," pronounced (aw-nawn'). It means cloud, cloudy, or cloud-mass. Cloud-mass is defined as a "theophanic cloud", in this definition. This cloud speaks of the glory of God.

The word "theophanic" comes from the word theophany, which is defined as a visible appearance of God in some form. It is also defined in history as the visible manifestations of the pre-incarnate Son of God. Examples of theophanies are the burning bush (Ex. 3:2), Jacob's vision at Bethel (Gen. 28:10-17), the pillar of fire and the pillar of cloud (Ex. 13:21) and Moses talking face-to-face with God (Ex. 33:11). The pillar of fire is defined as a supernatural fire, a theophany.

### The Glory in the House

The glory of God filled the tabernacle and appeared especially at the hour of sacrifice.

"And they brought [that] which Moses commanded before the tabernacle of the congregation: and all the congregation drew near and stood before the LORD. And Moses said, This [is] the thing which the LORD commanded that ye should do: and the glory of the LORD shall appear unto you." Leviticus 9:5, 6.

"Then a cloud covered the tent of the congregation, and the glory of the LORD filled the tabernacle. And Moses was not able to enter the tent of the congregation, because the cloud abode thereon, and the glory of the LORD filled the tabernacle. And when the cloud was taken up from over the tabernacle, the children of Israel went onward in all their journeys: But if the cloud were not taken up, then they journeyed not till the day that it was taken up. For the cloud of the LORD [was] upon the tabernacle by day, and fire was on it by night, in the sight of all the house of Israel, throughout all their journeys." Exodus 40:34-38.

Is the glory in the house? The house of God? Your house? Your temple? Your body? Is the glory in your house? I want to be where the glory is!

In the scripture above in Exodus 40, the glory filled the tabernacle, especially during the sacrifice. The church offers unto God a sweet smelling fragrance of the sacrifice of praise, and worship.

When the praises go up, the glory comes! When the praises go up, His presence comes! When the praises go up, the glory cloud comes down! When the praises go up, the message comes! When worship goes up, healing, deliverances, and victories take place!

God is raining glory in the house! God is raining glory upon his people in the midst of their praise. God is raining glory in His house! It's not raining only on the outside, but on the inside of us. The glory is filling the Lord's house across the land! Praises are going forth! Worship is ascending unto Him! Praise and worship are ascending, and the blessings of God are descending upon His people! Be thou glorified, O Lord in the midst of your glory! Christ in us the hope of glory! Be glorified O God in the midst of our intimate worship unto you!

Our hearts are exalted unto your throne. Our hands are raised to your Son! Our eyes are beholding your glory, high and lifted up, and filling all of the temple. Our ears are attuned to your voice! Our spirits are strong and filled from your fountain of glory! Our heads are lifted up and the King of Glory has entered our hearts.

"Lift up your heads, O ye gates; and be ye lift up, ye everlasting doors; and the King of glory shall come in. Who [is] this King of glory? The LORD strong and mighty, the LORD mighty in battle. Lift up your heads, O ye gates; even lift [them] up, ye everlasting doors; and the King of glory shall come in. Who is this King of glory? The LORD of hosts, he [is] the King of glory. Selah." Psalm 24: 7-10.

When the glory appears it is filled with God's honor, abundance, splendor, riches, wisdom, dignity, reputation, and His reverence. God is King of honor, King of glory, King of abundance, King of splendor, King of riches, King of wisdom, King of dignity, King of reputation, and King of reverence. When we worship, the King of glory appears in awesome ways! WORSHIP!

*Worship is like anesthesia. It takes you under
so that God can operate on your heart.*

*Praise to worship is like a caterpillar is to a butterfly.*

# CHAPTER TWENTY-TWO

# PASSPORT TO WORSHIP

"To preach the gospel in the regions beyond you." II Cor. 10:16

### A Place Called "BEYOND"

A passport is an official governmental document that certifies one's identity, citizenship, and permits a citizen to travel abroad. A passport gives one the right or privilege of passage, entry, or acceptance to a foreign land.

Think of being in this country as the normal, routine way of worshipping God. Think of getting a passport and leaving the country as going beyond the norm of worshipping God. Think of going to foreign lands as experiencing God in greater dimensions in worship. Going to foreign lands is going beyond in worship. So we get our passport to go to foreign, unknown, lands called "BEYOND". God has given us the right and privilege of passage, entry, and acceptance to unknown, new, higher, deeper, and greater dimensions of worship unto Him. Let's go the place in worshipping God called "BEYOND".

God does not want us to stay where we are in worship, but to inspire to experience deeper and higher heights in Him. God wants to take us beyond what we are customary to in worship! Our God is infinite, with infinite ways, and doings. The door is opened.

When I say beyond, I mean going pass what we know right now. Beyond is experiencing that which is pass our understanding, reach, knowledge, experience, and scope of worship. Beyond the worship we now experience is expressing worship somewhat to a greater degree than what is now. To take one beyond is to take one farther along, and away from the position, or place that we presently possess.

God wants to take us beyond in power, beyond in time (right out of time, into His presence), beyond in experience, beyond in knowledge, beyond in place, beyond in glory, beyond in scope, beyond in number, beyond in abundance, beyond in authority, beyond in what we have already perceived, beyond the yesterday and yesteryear of worship, beyond in what history has already portrayed! ONLY BELIEVE!.....And nothing shall be impossible unto you! God is infinite.

**Know that God is great, and greatly to be worshipped!**
Ask, and it shall be given you, seek and ye shall find, knock and the door will be opened unto you! And John looked, and behold the door was opened.

God wants us to desire to go beyond our ordinary responses to Him in worship, and travel to places in Him that we have never gone before, places that we have never seen, or walked before! Beyond the ordinary. Beyond the common. Beyond the average! Beyond the typical! Beyond the normal, and usual! Beyond what is commonly encountered! Beyond our imagination! Beyond our conception of worship! Beyond our concept, and definitions of worship! Beyond our boundaries. Beyond our limitations! Beyond our borders! Beyond guidelines, rules, policies, and traditions of worship! Beyond man's restrictions, and confinements! Beyond the margin! Beyond the lines!

Over the rim, pass the edge! Beyond our approaches! Beyond our determinations! Beyond our narrow-minded thoughts! Beyond our fixed thoughts of God and of worship! Beyond the extremes! Beyond the third dimension! Beyond measure! Beyond our thoughts, ideas, and ways in worship! Beyond our awareness of how we know to worship God! Beyond our insights, revelations, and knowledge of worship! God is infinite.

God wants to take us beyond what any human imagination, and human conception of what worship really is! God wants to take us into the unknown, foreign lands of worship, that we can only know by experiencing it ourselves; by encountering worship beyond ourselves.....by traveling into foreign lands, foreign territories, foreign waters, foreign distances, and foreign experiences that we have never experienced before. Get your passport....let's go....let's go to the place called "Beyond"....let's go into the unknown places in God....let's tap into the area of worship that's foreign to us....the unknown....that pleases God....PASSPORT WORSHIP!

How will we go beyond? What will permit us to cross the borderline of what we already know of worship? What will transport us beyond? Not by power, not by might, but by my spirit saith the Lord God. Where the spirit of the Lord is there is liberty. And ye shall know the truth, and the truth shall make you free.... Therefore, if the Son has set you free, ye shall be free indeed. Faith is the substance of things hoped for, the evidence of things not seen.

Your worship is limited right now. You are limited to a particular location, and place in God. God wants to set you free! God wants to loose you into other realms in Him. God wants you to go beyond your own restrictions, your own isolations, and worship Him in freedom, and liberty. God is infinite. "The zeal of the LORD of hosts shall perform this." Isaiah 9:7. Let's go beyond! Get your passport! Never return to mediocre worship ever again!

*Like the Word of God that penetrates every fiber of our being to the marrow of the bones, so worship penetrates my flesh transforming it from glory to glory to glory!*

*Like the rainbow, worship never ends.*

# CHAPTER TWENTY-THREE

# COME UP HITHER!

"....Come **up hither**, and I will shew thee things which must be hereafter." Revelation 4:1.

Come Up Hither! Ascend unto me. Are you ready for the flight? Ready for takeoff?

Ten...Nine...Eight...Seven...Six...Five...Four...Three...Two...One! Ready for take off! Have a nice flight!

It's time to arise! It's time to rise up and walk in the newness of life! It's time for greater sacrifice! It's time to reap abundance! It's time for a rich increase! It's time to mount up from the old way of doing things! It's time to grow up in the things of God! It's time for springing forth into new dimensions in God! It's time to launch out into the deep! It's time to branch out! It's time to take on a challenge that you only dreamed about in the pass. It's time to make the vision a reality! It's time for growth, and maturity! It's time to put away childish things! It's time to enter God's rest!

It's time to ascend higher in worship! It's time for exaltation! It's time for promotion! It's time to be lifted up! It's time for heighten experiences in God! It's time to walk by faith, or walk on the water!

It's time for advancement! It's time for high praise, and high glory! It's time for glorification! It's time for apotheosis! It's time for new dimensions, new levels, new heights, new plateaus, new realms, new experiences, and new growth in God! Come up hither! It's time to fly! Enjoy the flight!

Notice that the above verse of scripture does not say come hither interpreted come here. However, the verse declares to come **up** hither! This means that Jesus is standing waiting above where we are in Him. The expression "come up" literally means to go up, grow up, to ascend, mount up, rise up, or to come up. It is the Greek word, "anabaino", pronounced (an-ab-ah'ee-no). On the other hand, "hither" is defined as to come in this place, or to this place; to go there; or to come here.

Therefore, as you observe the entire phrase put together, you conclude that God is beckoning you to ascend to where He is. He is summoning you to come up to the spot where He is. He is not saying to come here, but to come up here! This is pointing out a particular direction, flight, or height that you must take. It is coming to a particular spot, or higher place in God.

The verse of scripture clearly indicates that Jesus is not located on the same level where John was; however, He is on a higher plane. This is the reason sometimes it appears that God cannot be found. It is because He has once again transcended to a higher place, and we not realizing it, think that God cannot be found or that He is not near, or is far away. No, He can be found, and He is not far away but He transcended to a higher realm, and is waiting on you. He waits to be found. He expects your arrival! He's waiting on you. Go to where He is, not where you want Him to be. "Seek ye the LORD while he may be found, call ye upon him while **he is near**." Isaiah 55:6.

As the apostle John in Revelation 4:1 heard the voice of God speak unto him, immediately he transcended in the Spirit, and began to see visions, and received revelations of God in a dimension that he had never seen or heard before this time. To John, he saw Jesus in a different dimension, since the last time he saw him before he ascended into heaven. All of this is symbolic of patterns that will transpire as we seek to transcend in the spirit to higher heights.

Prior to this scripture, in Revelation 3:20-22, Jesus is found knocking at the door of His own church. The door represents the hearts of the people. The door represents a barrier between them and the presence of God. God's presence was outside of the church. His presence was waiting and wanting to enter the church. His presence was trying to tap into His church for entrance. His presence was not in the church. The presence of God was missing on the inside. Behold, I stand at the door and knock.

The church on the inside was operating without Jesus. Oh, how dangerous! Therefore, everything was done in vain. All their efforts were futile. Jesus said".... For without me ye can do nothing." John 15:5. The only way to let Jesus in is to first have ears to hear what the Spirit is saying to the church. Jesus admonished if you would hear, then open the door, and He guaranteed that he would come in and sup, or dine with you.

Notice that in Revelation 4:1, the door in heaven was opened. John 10:7 and 9 states that Jesus is the door. "Then said Jesus unto them again, Verily, verily, I say unto you, **I am the door** of the sheep. **I am the door**: by me if any man enter in, he shall be saved, and shall go in and out, and find pasture." **Therefore, it is concluded that Jesus is the way, passage, or entrance into Himself. He is the entrance into the revelation of Himself.**

The opened door in Revelation 4:1 is a door of opportunity. Jesus was unveiling Himself. His door was opened unto John. His face was like an opened book, to be revealed, read, and understood. When we enter His door, we enter His character finding out more of Him. An opened door also depicts the opening, or unveiling of the scriptures. Remember that Jesus is the Word. John 1:1. Expect Him to unlock the revelation of His scriptures unto you.

The closed door in Revelation 3:20 versus the opened door in Revelation 4:1 have contrasting meanings. Jesus stated that if you open the door that He would come in and dine with you and you with Him. When the door is seen wide opened in Revelation 4:1, Jesus expects John to enter in and sup with Him.

The only way John enters in is through the spirit. The way or entrance into other levels is "**Not by might**, nor by power, but by my spirit, saith the LORD of hosts". Zechariah 4:6. If ye live in the spirit, walk in the spirit. Galatians 5:25. Walk by faith and not by sight. II Corinthians 5:7. So walking in the spirit is walking by faith! Soaring to higher dimensions is done by walking in the spirit, and by walking by faith.

Going up to, higher levels must be done in the spirit, walking by faith! The goal of transcending to higher heights is that Christ be fully formed in you.

Love is a large part of the picture. The more I learn to love, the more I grow! The more I grow, the more the fullness of Christ is formed, and fashioned within me. If I am immature, Christ has not been fully developed, or formed within me.

In some cases, He has been birthed, and is still a seed within us. **Immaturity stuns growth.** Immaturity hinders ascension in higher and greater things of God.

This is the reason why you must come up to different levels. So that Christ be fully developed in all His glory, and brilliance within you. The fullness of Christ blossoms where maturity is found, and love is complete. **You must grow up, to go up in Christ. It is imperative! Come Up Hither!**

Soar high to worlds unknown, to places in Christ that you have never gone before! Allow the Father to unveil, and reveal Himself. Allow the Father to impart revelation, wisdom, and strength into you. Exalt Him, and He will exalt you! Elevate Him, and He will elevate you. Honor Him, and He will honor you. "Be it far from me; for them that **honor me** I will honor, and they that despise me shall be lightly esteemed." I Samuel 2:30.

As you reach higher dimensions in Christ, there will never be a time when you can say that you have reached that ultimate, final plateau. Remember, these levels, and dimensions in Him are limitless! This is true because God is infinite. There is always another part of Him to be revealed to us. Rising to different dimensions in God deals with Christ being formed within you more and more. In addition, the scriptures are unveiled, and opened more and more unto you. The heavens are opened unto you to pour out more of Him.

In addition, ye shall increase more and more. "But we all, with open face beholding as in a glass the glory of the Lord, are changed into the same image from **glory to glory**, *even* as by the Spirit of the Lord." II Corinthians 3:18.

Come Up Hither! Come closer! Come Near! I bid you to come unto me! I welcome you! I beckon you to come! Come! Do enjoy your flight! You will never be the same! Rise up and soar! Rise up and fly! Come Up Hither!

*Worship is like the angels in Jacob's dream; it keeps ascending and descending.*

*Worship to a worshipper is like branches are to a vine. We die without it.*

*Worship is a wealthy place.*

# CHAPTER TWENTY-FOUR

# STANDING IN AWE OF GOD'S PRESENCE

"Let all the earth fear the LORD: let all the inhabitants of the world stand in awe of him." Psalm 33:8.

**These are the last days!** Now is the time that God is manifesting His presence in the earth like never before! God is showing Himself strong in the earth. "Let all the earth fear the LORD: let all the inhabitants of the world stand in awe of him." Psalm 33:8.

God is speaking loud, and clear! He is showing up, and manifesting Himself in the earth, around the world, to all nations, races, and peoples! He is showing up, and showing out!

He is showing Himself mightily in, and to individuals, including babies, children, teenagers, young people, the middle age, and to the older generations. "Out of the mouth of babes and sucklings hast thou ordained strength because of thine enemies, that thou mightiest still the enemy and the avenger." Psalm 8:2. And it shall come to pass in the last days, saith God, I will pour out my Spirit upon all flesh: and your sons, and your daughters shall prophesy, and your young men shall see visions, and your old men shall dream dreams: And on my servants and on my handmaidens I will pour out in those days my Spirit; and they shall prophesy." Acts 2:17,18.

He is manifesting Himself mightily in individuals, conferences, services, revivals, homes, businesses, schools, stores, etc., like never before! God is awesome! God is more than awesome! God is far, far, far more than awesome! **He's TERRIBLE!**

"How terrible art thou in thy works! Through the greatness of thy power shall thine enemies submit themselves unto thee!" Psalm 66:3. "Thou shalt not be affrighted at them: for the LORD thy God is among you, a mighty God and terrible." Deuteronomy 7:21. "Let them praise thy great and terrible name; for it is holy." Psalm 99:3.

Terrible means that God is exceedingly awesome! He is tremendously more than awesome! His name even is terrible! He is highly exalted, and reverence!

Now is the time in history, when God is showing Himself terrible in the midst of the congregation of His people! We stand in His presence, not knowing what to do! We stand in His midst being in awe of who He is, and who He is declaring Himself to be.

We are left speechless! We do not know whether to praise, or to worship. We do not know whether to bow, or to stand. We do not know whether to lie prostrate, or kneel before Him. We cannot help ourselves!

We sense His awesome touch, feel His awesome love, embrace His awesome power, and hear his awesome voice. We are left not knowing what to do. So we just stand—stand in awe of who He is—stand in awe of His greatness, His power, His love, His holiness, and His majesty!

His presence shows up, and it leaves us speechless! We have no ready response to responding to Him. He manifests Himself in a spectacular, supernatural, and divine way! We become overwhelmed by His presence! We become filled with His fulness! ".... And to know the love of Christ, which passeth knowledge, that ye might be filled with all the fulness of God". Ephesians 3:19.

We are filled with wonder, and amazement that He exceeds our perception of His greatness! We are filled with so much reverence for Him that we marvel ourselves of who He really is. We become baffled in His presence, overwhelmed in His fulness; overshadowed by His greatness, and His love!

His presence is so supernatural, so miraculous, so phenomenon, so remarkably astounding, so stupendous that we really do not know whether to raise our hands in the air, or whether to clap our hands. His presence is so unimaginable, extraordinary, and full of wonder, majesty, and power that we are left spell bound; we are caught up in His presence. We rapture right in His presence! You see, you do not have to wait on the rapture to experience it! Experience it in the presence of the Lord. Get caught up! Ascend unto Him! Meet Him!

Job was described this way, as God's presence was manifested to him. ".... Fear came upon him, and trembling, which made all his bones to shake. Then a spirit passed before his face; and the hair of his flesh stood up." Job 4:14.

Daniel said, "And he said unto me, O Daniel, a man greatly beloved, understand the words that I speak unto thee, and stand upright: for unto thee am I now sent. And when he had spoken this word unto me, I stood trembling." Daniel 10:11.

Habakkuk said, "When I heard, my belly trembled; my lips quivered at the voice...." Habakkuk 3:16.

John said, "And when I saw him, I fell as dead. And he laid his right hand upon me, saying unto me, Fear not; I am the first and the last:" Revelation 1:17.

Job also said, "At this also my heart trembleth, and is moved out of his place". Job 37:1.

Saul said, "And he trembling and astonished said, Lord, what wilt thou have me to do? Acts 9:6.

Belshazzar's reaction was, "Then the king's countenance changed, and his thoughts troubled him, so that the joints of his loins were loosed, and his knees smote one against another". Daniel 5:6. You see, God is TERRIBLE!

Therefore, these are a few reactions some have had from the presence, voice, word, or hand of God.

There is a part of God that is unsearchable! This part of God is called the 'noumenon' part of Him, that is, the part of Him that is indescribable.

God has parts of Him that is inexpressible! God is infinite. If I were to put that part of Him into words, there would be no words, or letters to formulate those expressions. You see, I am talking about the part of God that cannot be expressed between the A and the Z of our alphabet. No language can express this portion of God. No human, finite mind can even think about this portion of who God is. No scientist or mathematician can scientifically or mathematically, calculate this part of who God is, by using their experiments, their equations, their formulas, or by performing their own research for centuries. You see, this portion of God surpasses all understanding!

"For my thoughts are not your thoughts, neither are your ways my ways, saith the LORD. For as the heavens are higher than the earth, so are my ways higher than your ways, and my thoughts than your thoughts." Isaiah 55:8,9. "Call unto me, and I will answer thee, and shew thee the great and the mighty things, which thou knowest not." Jeremiah 33:3. "Now unto Him that is able to do exceeding abundantly above all that we ask or think, according to the power that worketh in us, unto Him be glory in the church by Christ Jesus throughout all ages, world without end. Amen". Ephesians 3:20, 21.

You can't figure out this part of God. You can't figure it out. You can't find it out. You can't think it out, because it is unknown to man. It is the higher thoughts, and the higher ways of God! It is the fact that He is infinite, and we are finite creatures. It is the things that He does that we know not of, and will never be able to figure it out! It is the exceeding, abundantly, above all that we can ask or think! God always has another way, another plan, another person, another thought, another method, another format, another design, another pattern, another cure, another healing, and another source, that we have no knowledge of. He is the way! John 14: 6.

Revelation 19:12 says that Jesus has a name written, that no man knows, but He himself. You can search baby name books, and books which gives the meaning of names, but never will any one of us on this earth come up with this name. There are parts of God that we have no knowledge of.

He exceeds awesomeness; and I stand in awe in His presence. "Let all the earth fear the LORD: let all the inhabitants of the world stand in awe of Him." Psalm 33:8. Let all of me fear the LORD, and stand in awe of Him.

Make yourself known to man, O God, that it may inspire worship like never before! Overwhelm us with your greatness! Declare unto us who you are, and who we are in you!

*Worship is our bouquet of flowers to the Father.*

*Kiss the Father with your worship.*

*Like the wise men that opened their treasures, and presented unto Jesus their best gifts: gold, frankincense, and myrrh; let us open the treasures in our earthen vessels and present the King of Kings with royal, pure, and holy worship! Give of your best!*

# CHAPTER TWENTY-FIVE

# A LETTER TO THE FATHER

As I lie prostrated before you Lord, let the words of my mouth and the meditation of my heart be acceptable in thy sight. For you are my strength, my redeemer, my savior, my all in all. Father, I desire you and you only. I yield to your power, your love, and your Spirit. Have your way, O Lord. Whatever your will is for me, your desires, your longings, your wants, your purpose, Lord, I beg you to perform them in my life.

Lord, I enter your gates with thanksgiving in my heart, and I come into your courts with praise. But I hear you Lord saying unto me, "Come unto me; come beyond my veil!" Lord, I am available to you. Here I am. I want to witness your glory, and your anointed presence, and your power in my life. I want to be changed, Father. Change me! Transform me! Lord, my earnest plea is that you bid me to come beyond your veil. I enter a new place in you, Father.

As I come beyond your veil, as I lay prostrate before you, I am experiencing your sweet love; your sweet touch; your sweet, tender, gentle voice; your sweet presence; your sweet, holy communion!

I hear you keep saying unto me Father, Come unto me.... Come beyond my veil.... Come in....Enter in. Come unto me. I hear you saying Lord, come closer, come nearer, so that we can be face to face.

I hear you saying Lord, I want to impart my seed within you; I want to touch you with my love. I want to be intimate with you. Come beyond the door. Come beyond my veil. Come unto me. Come. Enter in. Enter my dwelling place, my Most Holy Place, my secret place, oh, my place of love and oneness. Come unto me; abide with me; dwell with me; stay with me. Lie before me. Kneel before me. Bow before me. Thank me. Praise me. Worship me. Bless me. Minister to me. Commune with me.

So I say unto Lord, bid me to come unto you. Beckon me, Father. When I am lonely, troubled, depressed, and when I am in need of your love, overwhelm me with your love. Woo me. Call me. Whisper to me. Draw me in. Draw me into your presence. Bind me closer to you Lord. Hold me there Lord. Embrace, and show me your love. Overwhelm, and overshadow me with your love. Show me how to love you Father, as you love, adore, and cherish me. Surround me with your illuminating light, power, love, and truth. Earnestly, Father I yield to your call. I yield to your direction and correction in my life. I yield to your purpose in my life. I yield to your manifested power operating on my behalf. I yield to your will, and way. Lord, I desire to please you, above all others. Lord I desire to minister unto you. I want to bless you Father. I want to serve, and worship you Father. Father, oh, I love you. Show me your will. Thy kingdom come, thy will be done on earth as it is in heaven. Speak Lord, for thy servant heareth.

# ABOUT THE AUTHOR

Daphne Aleta Harris was born in Suffolk, Virginia to the late Dr. Ambrose E. Harris, Jr., and Mamie Ruth Harris, now residing in Portsmouth, Virginia. Mamie Ruth Harris is the mother of five sons, and two daughters, and is presently teaching school in Portsmouth, VA.

Daphne graduated from Manor High School in Portsmouth, Virginia in 1978. She was awarded a B.S. in Mathematics from Knoxville College, Knoxville, Tennessee, in 1982; a M.A. in Mathematics Education from the Ohio State University, Columbus, Ohio, in 1984; and a M.A. in Educational Administration from the Ohio State University, in 1996.

She also has attended Columbus Bible Institute, and the Eastern Union Bible College. Presently, Daphne teaches Algebra at Johnson Park Middle School, Columbus, Ohio where Marvenia E. Bosley is principal. She also is on staff at the Eastern Union Bible College located in Columbus, where Dr. E.A. Parham is President. Daphne's goal is to become a principal in one of the local schools soon.

Daphne responded to the call into the ministry as an evangelist, and teacher on April 17, 1991. Although she responded to the call in 1991, she taught, and spoke at a number of places before that time. Evangelist Harris is the founder of Crown Jesus Ministries, a ministry that helps in any walk of life, and seeks to crown Jesus with glory, and honor. Daphne is a member of Rhema Christian Center, Columbus, Ohio where LaFayette Scales is Pastor. At Rhema, Daphne teaches Praise & Worship in the Overcomers' Institute.

Daphne, being led by her father, received Jesus Christ as her personal Lord and Savior in December 1964, at age 5, and was baptized in the Ocean View River in the summer of 1971.

Daphne believes in giving God the glory for all things: her salvation, position in Christ, prosperity, and God's many blessings. Daphne, a lover of butterflies, scrabble, and computer technology, is a woman of change, a woman who is breaking traditional trends in her time. Her motto of her life is to praise God through the midst of blessings, and in any tribulations she encounters throughout all eternity.

**Worship ye the Lord!**

*Geraldine Dickerson*
*Praise God*

The author is proclaiming this good news in churches,
on campuses, and conferences.

Books may be ordered directly from the author.
Please send $9.99 + $3.95 to:

Daphne A. Harris
Crown Jesus Ministries
P.O. Box 9967
Columbus, Ohio 43209

**E-Mail Addresses:**
Queen D1@aol.com
daphar@freenet.columbus.oh.us

**Internet Address:**
http://www.columbus.k12.oh.us/johnson_park/harris.htm

**Fax Number:**
(614) 861-4928